Records and Recollections of
SIR WILLIAM PERKINS'S SCHOOL

1725 TO 2000

Records and Recollections of

SIR WILLIAM PERKINS'S SCHOOL

1725 TO 2000

GRESHAM BOOKS LTD
in partnership with
SIR WILLIAM PERKINS'S SCHOOL

© Sir William Perkins's School 2000

Published by
Gresham Books Limited
The Gresham Press
46 Victoria Road
Summertown
Oxford
OX2 7QD

In partnership with
Sir William Perkins's School

ISBN 0 946 095 38 8

Design and typesetting by John Saunders Design and Production
Jacket design by Ian Bottle
Printed and bound by MPG Books Ltd, Cornwall

ACKNOWLEDGEMENTS

I should like to express my thanks to the archivists and librarians of Chertsey Museum, Chertsey Library, The Surrey Records Office, The Guildhall Library, The Corporation of London Library, The Royal Archives at Windsor and The Tallow Chandlers Company for their help.

Permission was kindly given for the reproduction of

Documents: GU/29/2 and CC 47/1 in The Surrey Records Office
Photographs: No: 12 and 16 in Chertsey Museum
Drawing: TQ/043/670 of The Domestic Buildings Research Group

I am also grateful to the following authors and publishers for allowing me to use information from their work:

Avery, Gillian *The Best Type of Girl* , Andre Deutsch 1991
Briggs, Asa *How They Lived 1700 – 1815*, Basil Blackwell 1969
Burgess H J and Selsby P A *A Short History of The National Society 1811 – 1861*,published by The National Society
Chapman, Colin *The Growth of British Education and its Records* 2nd ed., Lochin 1996
Dean, E A and Pardoe, B *Curfew House: Historical Notes for the Domestic Buildings Research Group (Surrey) 1992*
Lander, J and Chapman, G *Historic Chertsey: A Guided Walk*, Prontaprint 1992
Littleboy, E J *Sir William Perkins's School: Famous Surrey Schools*, The Surrey County Magazine 1975

The unpublished notes of Sir John Brunner and work by members of the History Department have provided further information. I am particularly grateful to everyone who has contributed their memories of the school. Although it has not been possible to include all of them in this collection they are a valued addition to the school archives.

The idea of a short history of SWPS as part of the Millennium celebrations came from Susan Ross and I thank her for all the support she has given the project.

Anne Darlow

CONTENTS

Introduction

The remarkable survival of Sir William Perkins's School for 275 years is due to the local people who valued education and at different times helped to adapt the Foundation to meet changing needs.

The school's early history is difficult to chart. Legal records of the original Foundation and of later amendments were preserved but annual accounts and reports which would have given an insight into school life are for the most part missing. The first school master's book order in 1724 is one of the few primary sources to survive and it is fascinating for the light it sheds on what he taught, cost of materials and transport from London. One hundred years later the Charity Commissioners' Report gives another rare glimpse of conditions for children and teachers. By the latter part of the 19th century records were kept more systematically and when Sir John Brunner became Chairman of the Governors he assembled as much information as he could find about the school's history.

What follows here is simply a collection of extracts from documents, histories, school magazines and personal reminiscences with a commentary to bridge some of the gaps. It is inevitably unbalanced and heavily weighted with material from the 20th century. The past 50 years cannot yet be seen in perspective but personal recollections bring a colourful dimension to the school's story that is absent from the earlier eras. The sad discovery that information and images have slithered into oblivion even in recent years is a reminder of the importance of record keeping.

1 The inscription on the schoolhouse building in Windsor Street.

CHAPTER ONE
Sir William Perkins 1656?–1741

"He Died Immensely Rich"

THE EVENING POST
October 8th, 1741

'On Monday last died, at his seat in Chertsey in Surrey, Sir William Perkins, formerly an eminent Merchant of this City. He died immensely rich.'

THE LONDON DAILY POST
October 14th, 1741

'Last Night the Corpse of Sir William Perkins, Knt, who died the Beginning of last week at his House at Chertsea-Abby in Surry, in the 86th year of his Age, was, having lain there in State, carried from thence and interred with great Pomp in the Church-yard of St Mary-Axe; Sir William was drank to for Sheriff by the Lord Mayor of London in 1730, but afterwards paid his Fine.

His Lady, Dame Mary Perkins, who died September the 6th, Aged 75 Years, lies buried at Chertsea, where Sir William resided many Years; in his Lifetime, among other Charities, he erected a School there for the Education of 50 Boys and Girls, with a Sufficiency at his Death for a perpetual Maintenance of it. He is reported to have died worth £80,000 near half of which Sum has been found in his House, since his Decease.'

These newspaper reports of the death of Sir William Perkins reflect the success and standing he had achieved as a merchant in the City of London. Unfortunately only sparse details of his life story have survived the passage of time. He must have been born during the period of Cromwell's Commonwealth but his birth-place and early career are not known.

In 1689 he married Mary Alley, a widow of an East India Company merchant sea captain. She was already forty years old and there were to be no children of their marriage. However, it was at about this time that William Perkins' fortune was assured when he was appointed Purveyor of Wines and Surveyor of the Cellar to William III. He also secured the position of Clerk to the Board of the Green Cloth, a committee of the Royal Household which examined all its accounts. In 1695 he was elected to the Livery of the Tallow Chandlers Company, but he is described as a merchant. At one time he and others sold 'a carbuncle more valuable than a diamond' to the Crown for £12,000.

William Perkins was knighted in 1709 and of sufficient wealth and reputation to be nominated as Sheriff by the Lord Mayor of London in 1730. This was not quite the honour it might appear. Money was needed at the time to build the Mansion House and the names of several rich freemen of the City were put forward in the expectation that they would pay a heavy fine to avoid taking up the position.

The nephew who inherited Sir William's great fortune did not erect a memorial which might have provided more information about him. Instead his name has been kept alive as a result of the charity schools he founded in Chertsey.

CHAPTER TWO

Charity School 1725

By the beginning of the 18th century William Perkins was living in Chertsey. No doubt the condition of the children in the poor families he saw there prompted him to found a school for them: it was a generous and public spirited action. However, Sir William may also have shared the alarm, widespread among the merchant class of his day, that there was a dangerous and sharp decline in public morality. Their solution was to establish schools for the very poor, designed to 'promote social and godly discipline'. By 1730 one thousand, five hundred and sixty charity schools had been set up in England. The Society for the Promotion of Christian Knowledge was a principal sponsor and there was no shortage of publications and sermons offering advice on how they should be organised. Sir William would have been well informed and the schools at Chertsey followed the pattern of many others in their funding, curriculum and uniform.

GUIDANCE FOR CHARITY SCHOOLS

from 'An Essay towards the Encouragement of Charity Schools' – Isaac Watts 1728
'the schools should teach the children of the poor which are under their care to know what their station in life is, how mean their circumstances, how necessary t'is for them to be diligent, laborious, honest and faithful, humble and submissive, what duties they owe the rest of mankind and particularly to their superiors.'

from 'The Methods used to Erecting Charity Schools' – Pamphlet 1716
'the schoolmasters should be over the age of twenty three, understand well the principles of the Christian Religion, be of sober life and conversation, exercising good government of themselves and their passions, write a good hand and understand Arithmetic.'

from 'The Poor Girl's Primer'
'Make me dutiful and obedient to my benefactors and charitable to my enemies.
Make me temperate and chaste, meek and patient, true in all my dealings and content and industrious in my station'

from 'The Charity Spelling Book' by Mrs Sarah Trimmer
Moral Duties
Question: Is it honest for workmen to waste and destroy materials and implements which they make use of?
Answer: No
Question: Who do these things belong to?
Answer: The Master

Question: Whose eyes see you when your Master is not by?
Answer: God's

From 'How They Lived 1700 – 1815' by Asa Briggs 1969

The School House Building

Construction of the schoolhouse with two adjoining houses on either side began in 1723, twenty years after William Perkins had bought the land on the north side of Windsor Street. The work was to be completed for the sum of £1,000 by Edward Reeve, a builder of Twickenham, and a full specification of the construction and materials to be used has survived. Although progress on the schoolhouse was delayed by the death of Dame Mary Perkins, by 1725 it was ready. The school master, Isaac Knight, had been teaching twenty five boys somewhere since Christmas 1723 but now they moved into the handsome, purpose built school.

When Sir William extended the charity to twenty five girls in 1736, they and their schoolmistress, Mrs Coulsden, occupied House No: 16, next door but one to the schoolhouse.

(Report on Curfew House for the Domestic Buildings Research Group of Surrey by Mrs E A Dean and Mr Bernard Pardoe DBRG No: 2740)

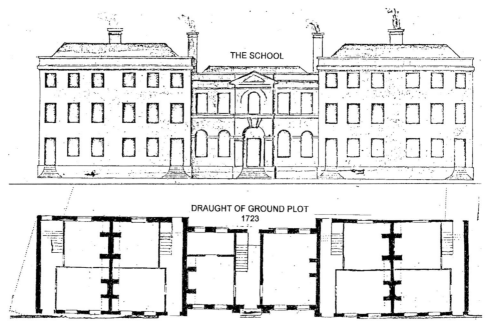

2 The ground plan and elevation of intended buildings, a schoolhouse and four houses, to be built for Sir William Perkins by Edward Reeves 1723. Courtesy of the Domestic Buildings Research Group TQ/043/670.

The School Master's Assessment and Book Order

The first schoolmaster appointed to Sir William Perkins's School was Isaac Knight. As early as February 1724, he had assessed twenty five boys and ordered the books and materials he needed from the Society for the Promotion of Christian Knowledge in London. The total cost, including transport by barge, was £5.19.10.

The present twenty five are qualified as follows:

8 that can read in a Bible are fit for writing

8 more can read in a Testament

9 others may learn at present in Spelling Books

An Estimate of what Books I may need y 1st year

25 Bibles with Common Prayer Books in them

12 Testaments

25 Spelling Books

25 Church Catechisms

25 Mr Lewis's Expositions

6 Doz.of Copy Books

1 Doz.of Blank Books for Cyphering

1 Doz. of Slates

1/2 Ream of Paper for use of the Children

1 Thousand of Quils pinnion

To be added

25 orders to be given to y parents of the children on their admission into the school being in half sheets.

To be sent to the Chertsey Barge at Queen Line On Tuesday morning for Will.m Sherly at The Naked Boy There

On the reverse

Surry		
Chertsey	4th Feb. 1724	
8.56. Sir William Perkins	Approv'd 19th Feb. Val	5.16-
Mr Weston Gov this to	Box and Post	3.10
H.N. 5th Feb. from		5.19.10
Sir Will. Perkins desiring the	Pd to H.N. 20th	
Society would allow the Books	Feb. 11	
within mentioned for the school	Mr Hoare and Mr Weston gave leave for	
he has open'd at Xmas last	sending the Books down 10. Feb. 1724	

Document G1/29/2 Surrey Records Office

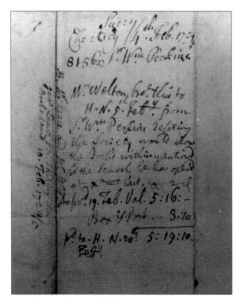

3 Assessment of the first 25 boys' reading skills and an order for books written by their schoolmaster 1724. Courtesy of the Surrey Records Office GU/29/2.

4 Reverse of book order showing the cost of materials and transport.

The Orders issued to Parents

The parents of each child admitted to the charity schools were given a list of Orders 'to be set up in their houses' – an early example of the home: school agreements.

ORDERS TO BE READ AND GIVEN TO THE PARENTS ON THE ADMITTANCE OF THEIR CHILDREN TO THE CHARITY SCHOOLS;AND TO BE SET UP IN THEIR HOUSES.

1 That the parents take care to send their children to school at the school hour, and keep them at home on no pretence whatsoever, except in case of sickness

2 That they send their children clean washed and combed

3 That in regard the trustees of this school will take due care that the children shall suffer no injuries by their master or mistress's correction, which is only designed for their good: the parents shall freely submit their children to undergo the discipline of the school, when guilty of any faults, and forbear coming thither on such occasions: so that the children may not be countenanced in their faults, nor the master or mistress discouraged in the performance of their duty.

4 That it is the duty of parents to keep their children in good order when they are at home, by good example and admonition.

5 That they teach their children at home their catechism, and read the Holy Scriptures, especially on the Lord's Day, and use prayers morning and evening in their families; so that both parents and children may be better informed of their duty, and by a constant and sincere practice thereof procure the blessing of God upon them.

6 That the children attend the Parish Church on the Lord's Day (commonly called Sunday), both in the morning and afternoon, and holidays, Wednesdays and Fridays; and that the master and mistress respectively take notice of their behaviour, and of those who shall be absent at any of those times.

7 That the parents do not take their children out of school, without first obtaining leave of the trustees; and whatever child shall be so removed without leave, before that time, shall not have clothes or books, nor any other child of those parents taken into the schools.

8 If the parents do not observe the said orders, their children are to be dismissed the school, and to forfeit their school clothes.

Ye fathers provoke not your children, to wrath, but bring them up in the nurture and admonitions of the Lord: having them in subjection with all gravity. Eph.vi.4., Tim.iii.4

Honour thy father and thy mother that it may be well with thee, and thou mayest live long on the earth. Eph.vi.2-3

from 'Growth of British Education and its Records' by Colin Chapman

The Curricula and Funding of the Schools

The girls' curriculum was significantly narrower than that of the boys and the schoolmistress was paid far less than the schoolmaster. For clothes, coals and repairs the allowances were the same.

Sir William Perkins, Knight, residing at Chertsey, in 1725 built a schoolhouse on the North side of the street called Windsor Street in that Town, and placed therein a school-master to teach 25 poor boys of that Parish reading, writing, arithmetic and the Catechism of the Church of England, and Sir William also clothed the boys.

In 1736 Sir William extended his munificence by building another house for a school for 25 girls and a schoolmistress. The girls to be taught reading, the Catechism of the Church of England and plain work: to be of the Parish of Chertsey, if the Trustees found so many in their discretion fit to be admitted, otherwise to be taken out of the three adjoining Parishes of Thorpe, Egham and Chobham.

He declared the trusts of the two said houses ...and of £3,000 of Bank Stock to be settled as maintenance for the said schools viz. as to £75 a year, to pay thereout a salary of £25 a year to the master, £25 a year to be applied to clothe the boys at Easter,

5 The former schoolhouse in Windsor Street after a third storey had been added - from a painting by J. Hassell in 1832 presented to the school by Sir John Brunner.

£10 for coals and books, and £15 for repairs or other uses for support of the schools or relating thereto, as the Trustees for the time being should think necessary; and after satisfying the said £75 a year to apply £15 for the salary of the schoolmistress, £25 for clothing the girls at Easter, £10 for coals and books, and the residue of the rents as income for repair of the girls' school and for other uses for support of both or either of the two schools.

from 'The History of Surrey. Vol, 111' by Manning and Bray 1804 – 1814

The Charity School Day

The daily routine and uniform of Sir William Perkins's School were probably similar to those recorded for other charity schools in the 18th century.

In the girls' school the first two hours were devoted to religious studies and reading lessons. They were not taught writing and arithmetic like the boys so they passed the remainder of the day in 'industrial occupation'. This meant long hours of sewing as the schoolmistress usually took in work from the local community for which a suitable charge was made. The girls also stitched many items of their own uniform and knitted and mended their yellow stockings.

The uniform was chosen for its durability and suited to the children's lowly status. It was not intended to be worn with pride but as an indication that they came from the poorest families in the parish.

The girls' dress was of blue serge: gowns open in front, showing a petticoat also of blue serge. The low square neck was bound with yellow and the straight sleeves had a yellow band at the wrist. In summer white linen tippets and white linen caps with crimped borders were added. They wore blue and white checked aprons, hand knitted yellow stockings and heavy nailed boots, and their underwear they made themselves.

For church, plain straw bonnets with blue ribbon tied under the chin were worn over the caps, and they also had long cotton mittens.

In winter they were provided with warm grey cloaks, and they wore on the breast a brass oval medal with their own special number.

The boys wore shirts of stout linen, leather breeches and short jackets, woollen caps with a tassel, yellow stockings and thick metal tipped boots

E J Littleboy, from 'Famous Surrey Schools', The Surrey County Magazine, June 1975

In these distinctive uniforms the pupils marched in procession along Windsor Street to St Peter's Church every Sunday, Christmas Day, Good Friday and Ash Wednesday. They sat down the centre of the church under the watchful eye of the

6 The Charity School uniform – without the boots!

schoolmaster who had his seat below the pulpit. There too they could be seen by prospective employers who might offer the boys a trade or craft apprenticeship and the girls a situation in which they could use their sewing skills.

A 1795 town directory of Chertsey noted that 'The Charity School is a very good one' but already by that time support for the kind of education offered in such schools was declining.

The process of change was accelerated in Chertsey by the appointment in 1795 of four new trustees to Sir William Perkins's Charity. A prolonged case had been won in the Court of Chancery against absentee trustees who had neglected their obligations. In contrast their successors, all parishioners of Chertsey, were energetic in planning improvements for the schools.

CHAPTER THREE
Voluntary Elementary School 1819

By 1819 the new school trustees had set afoot momentous changes for Sir William Perkins's School. These sprang mainly from the needs of the growing population of Chertsey. While there were two academies for young gentlemen and another for young ladies, the school rooms in Windsor Street were by now dilapidated and quite inadequate for all the children of poor families. For once the financing of change was not a major problem: the investments supporting Sir William Perkins's Charity produced a handsome surplus.

The trustees devised a scheme to extend and improve the schools and by 1818 it had been approved by the Court of Chancery. They were given permission to sell the Windsor Street houses and to build new schools on a one and a half acre site at the end of Guildford Street. These would accommodate up to 225 poor boys and 100 poor girls from Chertsey or the adjoining parishes. This timely modification of the charity gave virtually all the local children access to education more than sixty years before free schooling became government policy.

The indenture of 1819 made another radical change: Sir William Perkins's Schools were to adopt the 'National System' which had originally been devised by Dr Alexander Bell in Madras to educate the orphans of soldiers. He had since established The National School Society which aimed:

'To bring about the gradual improvement of the state of the poor by training their children in the principles of virtue and true religion, by instructing them in those elementary branches of learning which are requisite to their stations and by placing it in their power to contribute essentially to the comfort and support of their parents and to become useful, happy and respectable themselves.'

For some time the trustees considered affiliating the schools to the National Society but instead they decided only to use its system of education. The solution it offered to the problem of providing teachers was its strongest recommendation.

By far the largest item in any school's budget was the teacher's stipend. In 1820 the salary of the master at Sir William Perkins's Schools had risen to £70 a year and that of the schoolmistress to £40. The only way the increased number of children could be taught was by 'mutual instruction' as used in the National System.

Children who had been instructed in the rudiments of a subject by the master in turn taught classes of their own. Each class had up to forty pupils, selected by ability rather than by age, with its child teacher appointed from the class above and an assistant child teacher from its own ranks.'

In the following extract from the Charity Commissioners' Reports it was these child teachers who were rewarded at Christmas with one shilling each. The help of the National Society was also sought in replacing the schoolmaster and schoolmistress.

STAFF APPOINTMENTS AND PUPILS REWARDS AT
SIR WILLIAM PERKINS'S SCHOOL 1819 – 1821

In consequence of the total incapacity of the then master, application was made to the National School in Baldwin's Gardens for a training master; and in April 1819, Charles Bartlett was sent down, who received a salary of £2 2s per week, that being the usual allowance paid to training masters. Mr Bartlett having died suddenly on the 24th July 1819, Mr Bond was, on a fresh application to the National Society in Baldwin's Gardens, sent down the 22nd of August following.

The boys and girls were removed to the new school at Michaelmas 1819 and Mrs Oliphant was appointed mistress at the recommendation of the National Society, at a salary of £40 a year, ordered by the Court of Chancery. The trustees not being able to obtain a clergyman, as ordered by the Court, for a master, determined at Christmas 1820, to agree with Mr Bond to take the situation of permanent master, at a salary of 70 guineas per annum; the trustees promising to give him three months notice, if at any time thereafter a clergyman should be appointed to instruct the children.

At a meeting of the trustees held in April 1821, the treasurer reported that in the preceding 12 months, 52 boys had been admitted, 19 had quitted, and 132 remained in the school; 25 girls had been admitted, 10 had quitted, and 81 remained in the school; 45 boys and 28 girls had been rewarded at Christmas 1820, for constant attendance at school; and the five best boys, and the five best girls, in each class, according to their weekly order, were rewarded with 6d each, and the teachers of each class with 1s each. That two boys and three girls, who had behaved well while in the school, had received £2 each for clothing on going into service, and one boy an apprentice fee of £5. That four girls had received £1 each, for having behaved well during one year in service.

from 'The Charity Commissioners' Reports 1824'

The girls must have welcomed the improvements Mrs Oliphant introduced in their curriculum. Although they were still taught to sew and knit they now had access not only to reading, but writing and ciphering like the boys. Religious exercises, of course, remained the first priority for all the pupils. A number of the poorest children were still clothed from the Foundation funds but the unpopular charity school uniform was abandoned. The only reference in the records to the children's clothes comes in later reported complaints from the schoolmaster and schoolmistress who objected to the smell that emanated from the children's cloak-rooms and permeated their houses. This 1842 description of the school buildings on the new site also records a rise in the pupil numbers since 1819.

CHERTSEY FREE SCHOOL

The present school house, which is a large plain building of light coloured brick with a slated roof, is situated at the southern extremity of Guildford Street. It was erected by contract in 1819, at the cost of £2,898. 11s 11d. including the purchase of the ground. The apartments respectively appropriated to the master and the mistress are in front; and each has the benefit of a small garden. The school room which is on the upper floor, is very spacious and divided by a cross partition into two distinct apartments for the boys and for the girls; they have also detached play-grounds, and a space at the back is covered in for their use in wet weather. The total number of boys at present receiving instruction here is one hundred and fifty-nine; of girls one hundred and twenty; of whom forty boys and thirty five girls are clothed as well as educated.

From 'A Topographical History of Surrey' by Edward Wedlake Brayley 1842

The use of the National System solved some of the problems but its shortcomings were recognised at the time. Most of the learning was by rote and the noise of several classes chanting different lessons in a single schoolroom can be imagined. Few children advanced beyond the most basic level of education. Standards only improved gradually in the second half of the 19th century as pupil teachers were selected for the newly established training colleges. As late as 1878 the schoolmaster at Sir William Perkins's School had only one ex-pupil teacher and two monitors to help him teach some 200 or so boys.

The first trained Assistant Teachers were appointed to the school in 1882 soon after the Charity Commissioner has approved a scheme with ten governors to administer the Foundation in place of the three trustees. These new governors decided that fees had to be raised to help pay the higher salaries due to qualified staff but even the 2d a week for each infant and 3d for an older child imposed a burden many local parents could not bear. In any case poor families were glad of the

7 The National Schools - a sketch made from a painting by J Hassell in 1832 presented to the school by Sir John Brunner.

few pennies young children might earn in simple farm work and non attendance at school was a major problem.

The annual grant from the Government was determined by the attendance records and the report from Her Majesty's Inspector. This was particularly important to Sir William Perkins's School which received no help from the local rates because it was a voluntary school.

Sensibly the governors adopted the carrot rather than the stick approach by offering decorative certificates to those children who came to school regularly. They even promised a nickel watch to any child who completed three years without absence though there is no record that anyone ever qualified for one.

Regular attendance remained important but the system of 'payment by results' and fees ended in 1890. The change of policy was timely. In that year unemployment was causing acute hardship in Chertsey and the headmaster recorded in the school log book that he had collected subscriptions to provide breakfasts for boys whose fathers were out of work.

The government grant for each child at Sir William Perkins's School was twenty shillings and sixpence in 1891 but the Foundation funds that had seemed comfortably sufficient at the beginning of the century were now severely stretched.

In the circumstances it is remarkable how much the Governors achieved to meet new laws and to satisfy local demands. Forster's Education Act of 1870 required all children to attend school from the age of five so money from the Foundation Fund was used to rebuild and enlarge the Windsor Street Infants School and to build a new infants department on the Guildford Road site. Although this meant that the Governors could not meet requests for a 'higher education' school, they did establish extra fee paying classes in which boys and girls could study new subjects: Geography, History, Drawing, Vocal Music and French. They provided a library and a Giant Stride in the playground. The latter proved so popular with some of the boys that the headmaster found them playing on it at 6.00am! By 1892 a laboratory, new classrooms and a gymnasium were under construction to serve not only the school but evening classes. Working people could learn technical, commercial, language and domestic skills. Specialist teachers were recruited, including a 'military man' for the gymnasium, and arrangements were made for the visit of a dairy van for instruction in butter making.

In 1973 Mrs Eileen Schumacher recorded some of her mother's recollections of Sir William Perkins's School in the 1880's.

The school took both boys and girls – the boys on the first floor, the girls on the ground floor. The gym was used by the boys and girls. It had a horse for vaulting; rings on ropes for swinging exercises and it was the finest in equipment of any school in 1908. The headmistress in the 1880's when my mother was a pupil was Mrs Eden and she had a house provided on the school site. Mr Bailey was headmaster of the boys and also taught my mother French. Pupils paid 1d a week extra for lessons. The inspector came annually to test the pupils and this was quite as exacting an ordeal as taking O Levels and A Levels. Mrs Eden wanted my mother to train as a school teacher but her mother, because of the Needlework Prize, insisted that she was apprenticed to a Court dressmaker, Mrs Bannerman, in Chertsey. In those days ornate Victorian dresses were made to last for generations and were works of art.

In 1887 Miss Schumacher's mother might have taken part in the Jubilee celebrations that marked the 50th year of Queen Victoria's reign. A special treat was organised for the pupils of Sir William Perkins's School by one of their governors, Mr Frank Taylor. Paying tribute to their 'beneficent donor and founder', six hundred children lined up in procession at the school, then marched through the town carrying a great banner inscribed ' Good Sir William Perkins.' The long column eventually wound its way up St Anne's Hill and there 'the rest of the day was enjoyed with games, tea, prize-giving and speech making'. The junior forms

8 Certificate for success in the 5th standard examination presented to Sarah Atkins in 1904.

continue the tradition to this day by marching up to St Anne's Hill each summer to celebrate the end of their examinations.

A hundred years ago there was the same sense of relief after the annual examinations by Her Majesty's Inspector but then the whole school was given a day's holiday. There was another day off for the Chertsey Fair and for the annual visit of the circus, and all the children were let out of school to welcome the arrival of Chertsey's first fire engine in 1890.

Amy Elizabeth Bennett was a pupil from 1895 to 1903:

I have very happy memories of my schooldays. I remember my teacher whom I liked was named Miss Fairmanner. As I was good at needlework, I made her by hand a set of underwear, nightdress, chemise, knickers. I believe the headteacher was named Miss Ayres. It was about 1903 or 1904 when I left school. My sister, two years younger, was there at the same time.

9 Certificate for a full term's attendance presented to Beatrice Barnett in 1904.

10 Sampler embroidered by Mary A Wood in 1870.

I remember when I left I had just passed some exams and was second from the top. When we took our exams we were always moved to sit in different places.

Sometimes gentlemen took the lessons. We used to march to the gymnasium for drill, dumb bells, bar pole, etc. Tennis was in the recreation ground. I remember going to King Edward's Coronation Sports. I won six prizes.

Agnes Dorothy Joyner (nee Clench) was at Sir William Perkins's School from 1899 to 1907

My home was at Lyne Level Crossing Gates, where my father was signalman. We had quite a journey's walk to Sir William Perkins's School, and always had to take sandwiches for our dinner. At one time we were four girls going to school.

My first school days were at the Infant's School. And our teachers were the two Miss Garretts. From there I went on to the big girl's school where the headmistress was Miss Walker. She lived in the school building. She unfortunately was drowned whilst on holiday in Scotland.

I enjoyed school very much although I was naughty sometimes. At the side adjoining our school was the Boys' School. The headmaster was Mr Bailey.

One highlight I remember was that every week if we made a full attendance, we were given a picture postcard of special places and buildings in Surrey. I was seldom absent so I had many such cards. I especially enjoyed the Physical Training Lesson in the gymnasium. On the right hand side of the school was a field where once a year a fair was held, but we were never allowed to go to it. Our parents did not like us to do so.

Sometimes in the winter the roads were flooded and we had to travel another way to school and were picked up by a driver with a horse and cart, and put down over the Bourne Bridge and walked to Windsor Street along Guildford Street, over the Station Bridge and on to Guildford Road and so on to school. Otherwise our journey took us past the Golden Grove, and the Grange, through Lasswade Road, along Goosepool where many Italians lived, and so over the Railway Bridge to school.

My dear father died very suddenly on April 16th, 1907, just before my thirteenth birthday, so we had to move and went to live in Lyne, so unfortunately I had to leave Sir William Perkins's School and went to finish my education at Lyne School.

CHAPTER FOUR

School Closure 1908

Her Majesty's Inspectors looked at Sir William Perkins's School with a trained critical eye and by the late 1890's their reports were peppered with adverse comments. For some time the school had been languishing for lack of sufficient funds and the crisis came to a head in 1902.

Special Meeting of the Governors held on January 9th 1902 to consider the Report of H M Inspector, Mr J C Colvill

Mr Colvill reported that he considered the present state of the schools, especially the teaching, most unsatisfactory. A committee of Governors was appointed to give careful and anxious consideration to 'The Grave deficiencies of Discipline, Organisation and Instruction'.

In the face of such harsh criticism the Head Teachers must have attended the personal interviews to which they were summoned with some trepidation. In fairness to them the committee recognised that 'the Head Teachers were saddled with the responsibility of teaching large classes themselves and had not been able to exercise strict supervision over the staff and scholars, nor over the methods of procuring discipline and of giving instruction.' Nonetheless the list of recommendations gives some idea of what had been going wrong. The Head Teachers were exhorted to make some effort to establish a better feeling of mutual respect and esteem between themselves and their staff, and in turn between the whole staff and the scholars. They were not to be absent during school hours; they alone should deliver and record corporal punishment and all members of staff were to be present a quarter of an hour before school began to have all in readiness. An annual report as to the work and position of the scholars was to be made.

To their credit the Governors agreed to appoint more staff to free the Head Teachers from some teaching, but the headmistress, Miss Eden, handed in her notice the following year. By that time another serious crisis was looming and the Governors would be forced to admit that many of the school's problems could not be resolved as long as it occupied the 1819 buildings.

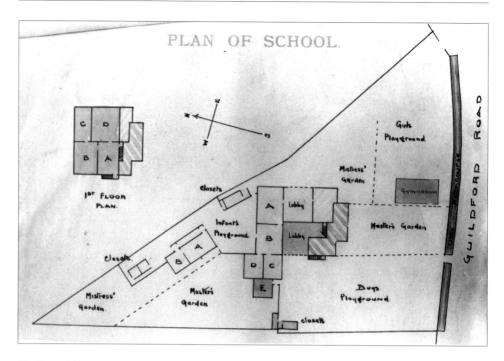

11 Plan of Sir William Perkins's Voluntary School in the Surveyor's Report of 1904. Striped area: houses of schoolmaster and schoolmistress. Ground floor: Girls' classrooms. First floor: Boys' classrooms. Infants' classrooms, gymnasium, laboratory E all built in 1892/3. Courtesy of Surrey Records Office CC/47/1.

Sir William Perkins's Voluntary School Surveyor's Report May 1904

This building is of a very unsatisfactory character inasmuch as the original portion of the building is necessarily antiquated and not at all in accordance with the requirements of a modern elementary school. I have no hesitation in saying that the best plan would be to demolish the main building altogether.

The surveyor supported this recommendation with some alarming evidence. At the time of his visit he had found 94 boys in one classroom and 108 girls in another. There were open fires without guards, poor lighting, a stuffy atmosphere, wooden floors that resounded in the rooms above and below whenever children moved about. There was no means for the Head Master to supervise what was going on. Outside the cess pool overflowed into the boys' playground and thence into the water course along the Guildford Road into which children had fallen on several occasions. The lavatories were totally inadequate and two wash basins served 270 girls.

The report precipitated action. The Governors quickly produced improvement plans but Surrey Education Committee took the view that repairs and adaptation would still leave the buildings unsuitable for use as Public Elementary Schools. Instead they proposed transferring responsibility for the existing schools to the Local Education Authority so that the Perkins's Charity could be used for the advancement of higher education in Chertsey. Government encouragement had been given in the 1902 Education Act and by 1906 it had been agreed to 'establish a secondary school for girls of the same nature as that proposed to be established in Egham for the administration of the Strode's Charity.'

The old schools were officially closed on July 29th 1908. In the registers for that day were the names of 269 boys, 298 girls and 118 infants. At the end of the summer holidays the children and most of the staff moved on to the new Council schools on the Stepgates site. It was the close of an era and no more boys were to be educated at Sir William Perkins's School, a fact much regretted by many of its later pupils.

A photograph taken in 1910 from the recreation ground shows the old elementary school buildings before the demolition teams did their work. Two years later only the 1893 infants department and the gymnasium were left standing. The former survived until 1999 and the gymnasium building remains to this day.

12 Photograph of the SWP Voluntary Elementary School taken from the Recreation Ground in 1910. The infant classrooms are on the left and the roof of the gymnasium to the right at the rear. Courtesy of Chertsey Museum.

13 Miss Eastaugh with the staff and first 46 girls of the SWP Foundation Secondary School for Girls 1914.

CHAPTER FIVE

Secondary School for Girls

For six years there was no Sir William Perkins's School. The long interval between the closure of the old school and the opening of the secondary school for girls was needed for financial and administrative reasons. The income from the Sir William Perkins's Foundation began to accumulate in a fund for the new building only when the County had taken over responsibility for the elementary schools. Meanwhile new rules for management had to be agreed and the scheme only received final government approval in March 1910.

Three months later the newly constituted Board of Governors met for the first time in the former infants' classroom on the Guildford Road site. There were 17 members including representatives from Surrey County Council and the University of London. By good chance Sir John Brunner, co founder of ICI, had retired to Chertsey and he was elected Chairman. Through his generosity a further two and a half acres of land was acquired as a playing field in 1912.

By this time the building work had begun and the school was constructed at a cost of £8,000. Early in 1914 an advertisement in the local paper invited people to inspect its fine, modern facilities. The governors appointed Miss Eastaugh as headmistress though she was only twenty nine years old. With her three staff colleagues and their first 46 pupils they posed for a celebratory photograph just a few weeks after Sir William Perkins's Secondary School for Girls had opened.

'THE FIRST FOUR'
These are the teachers seated in the 1914 photograph.

Miss Mabel Eastaugh – Headmistress
   29 years old.
   Educated at Tottenham Girls' High School and Royal Holloway College
   Previously Science Mistress at Guildford County School
   To organise the work of the school.
   Special subjects: Mathematics and Chemistry
   Teacher of Mathematics and Drill throughout the school.
   Salary £200 p.a.

Miss Winifred Slater
   28 years old.
   Educated at Tottenham Girls' High School and Newnham College,
   Cambridge.
   Teacher's Training Certificate.
   Special subjects: French and German
   To organise and teach French throughout the school.
   Teach also Divinity, Writing, Needlework.
   Salary £120 p.a.

Miss Sydney Elizabeth Swaffield
   26 years old.
   Educated at Cork High School for Girls and University College, Cork.
   Teachers' Diploma
   Previously at Kinnaird Park School in Bromley.
   Special subjects: Chemistry, Physics, Mathematics, Geography
   To organise and teach Science and Geography throughout the school and
   teach some Arithmetic, Needlework and Games.
   Salary £120 p.a.

Miss Florence Maud Davy
   25 years old.
   Educated at Kensington High School, GPDST, and Royal Holloway College.
   Previously at Leek Church High School
   Special subject: History
   To organise and teach History and English throughout the school and teach
   some Divinity, Needlework, Arithmetic and Games.
   Salary £110 p.a.

From The Staff Register: April 1914

Four part-time teachers were also employed to teach Gardening (£5 p.a.) Class
Singing (£12 p.a.) Drawing (£20 p.a.) and Swedish Gymnastics (10s. 6d an hour)

The 1914 School Register

The first school register lists the names and details of the 46 girls in the 1914 photograph. Their descendants might still be able to put a name to a face but a pre First World War society is reflected in their ages, previous schools – or lack of one, and fathers' occupations. War itself must have been responsible for the brevity of many school careers. The occupations the girls themselves entered were in some cases open to women for the first time because so many men were in the armed services.

	Name	Date of Birth	Previous School	Father's Occupation	Time at Sir William Perkins's School	Later Career
1	Doris Lilley	25.11.1900	Addlestone High	Tobacconist	1914 - 1917	Bank Clerk
2	Georgina Jessop	21.2.1901	Ashford County	Head Gardener	1914 - 1916	Munitions Worker
3	Doris Stephenson	6.5.1900	Tiffins, Kingston	Non Conformist Minister	1914 - 1915	Leeds University
4	Blanche Nicholson	17.10.1902	None	Chemist	1914 - 1920	Furzedown Training College
5	Margaret Nicholson	5.9.1905	None	Chemist	1914 - 1922	Photography
6	Kathleen Boullin	26.11.1900	Ottershaw Elementary	Dairyman	1914 - 1915	Clerk in the Counting House
7	Audrey Boullin	12.9.1901	Ottershaw Elementary	Dairyman	1914 - 1917	Dispensing
8	Florence Corps	13.2.1901	Lyne Elementary	Motor Trimmer	1914 - 1915	Clerk in the Post Office
9	Pepita Cerda Saunders	4.11.1902	Private School Weybridge	Company Director	1914 - 1915	Adelaide University
10	Ellen Jones	18.6.1899	Private School Chertsey	House Agent	1914 - 1915	Assistant in Father's Business
11	Phyllis Wasley	16.7.1899	Virginia Water Elementary	Head Gardener	1914 - 1915	Clerk in the Post Office
12	Mabel Collis	23.7.1899	St Lawrence Elementary	Deceased	1914 - 1917	Elementary Teacher
13	Lily Allen	26.4.1900	Tiffins, Kingston	Saddler	1914 - 1916	Somerset House
14	Marjorie Dell	11.2.1902	Longcross Elementary	Farm Steward	1914 -1918	Bank Clerk
15	Alice Crouch	22.1.1900	Ottershaw Elementary	Butler	1914 - 1916	Army Pay Clerk

16	Nora Smith	2.11.1899	St Judes Elementary	Grocer's Assistant	1914 - 1915	Cashier in Grocery Business
17	Cecilie Knight	12.9.1900	Stepgates Elementary	Deceased	1914 - 1915	?
18	Hilda Matthews	3.8.1900	Addlestone High	Manager of Gas Works	1914 - 1915	Elementary Teacher
19	Ivy King	1.12.1899	Englefield Green Elementary	Carpenter	1914 - 1916	Clerk in Post Office
20	Muriel Cobley	26.6.1900	None	Railway Clerk	1914 - 1916	?
21	Florence Harnett	14.4.1900	Stepgates Elementary	Draper	1914 - 1915	Draper's Apprentice
22	Marjorie Roake	15.4.1899	St Maur's Convent	Blacksmith	1914 - 1916	Clerk, Chertsey Council
23	Elizabeth Farmer	25.9.1898	Tiffins, Kingston	Draper	1914 - 1915	Fashion Designer
24	Grace Norris	19.2.1900	Stratford House, Sunninghill	Head Gardener	1914 - 1918	East London College
25	Mary Wells	20.2.1901	Stepgates Elementary	Builder	1914 - 1916	Clerk in War Office
26	Monica Wilson	25.4.1900	Eastworth House Convent	Steward	1914 -19 16	Clerk in Motor Works
27	Edna Jago	8.11.1902	Eastworth House Convent	Pharmacist	1914 - 1920	St Gabriel's Training College
28	Joan Hamilton	25.6.1902	None	Secretary to Gas Works	1914 - 1920	Photographic Studio
29	Jean Hamilton	1.2.1901	None	Secretary to Gas Works	1914 -1919	Guildhall School of Music
30	Viola Ellis	13.11.1902	Worthing High	Poet	1914 - 1917	Royal School of Music
31	Hilda Stevens	14.1.1900	Tiffins, Kingston	Solicitor's Clerk	1914 - 1917	Clarke's College
32	Lucy Thomas	9.2.1903	Private School Chertsey	Coach Builder	1914 -1920	Clarke's College
33	Kathleen Brown	12.4.1901	St Paul's Addlestone	Butcher	1914 - 1915	Tiffins Kingston
34	Ethel Sale	27.1.1901	Ottershaw Elementary	Coachman	1914 - 1916	?
35	Kathleen Evans	19.5.1896	Worthing High	Deceased	1914	King's College London
36	Iris King	19.11.1901	Englefield Green Elementary	Carpenter	1914 - 1917	Clerk
37	Lydia Thomas	12.5.1901	Miss Wheeler's	Coach Builder	1914 - 1918	Goldsmith's Training College

38	Ivy Townsend	2.10.1905	Miss Mortlock's	Farmer	1914 - 1919	St Catherine's Bramley
39	Agnes Grant	16.2.1905	None	Captain in Royal Navy	1914 -1917	School in Horsell
40	Lilian Warinton	15.11.1900	Stepgates Elementary	Iron Moulder	1914 -1916	Clerk in Garage
41	Hilda Hanney	5.1.1902	Stepgates Elementary	Telegraphist Sorting Clerk	1914 - 1919	Uncertificated Teacher
42	Mary Waspe	27.4.1902	Longcross Elementary	Coachman	1914 -1918	Clerk in Propellor Works
43	Dorothy Waffendale	31.3.1901	Littleton Elementary	Commercial Traveller	1914 - 1917	?
44	Margaret Copland	29.9.1902	Longcross Elementary	School Master	1914- 1918	Clerk in Propellor Works
45	Hilda White	9.11.1901	Weybridge Elementary	Works Clerk	1914 - 1919	Pensions Office Clerk
46	Barbara Bates	28.10.1904	Highfield Private School	Boat Builder	1914 - 1922	Apprenticed Messrs Hardings

SURREY HERALD and EGHAM & STAINES NEWS
July 24th, 1914

CHERTSEY'S SECONDARY SCHOOL

Formally Opened –
Interesting Speeches

After the additional facilities for education afforded by the Sir Wm. Perkins's Secondary School for girls have been enjoyed by nearly fifty pupils for a term, the institution was 'formally' opened on Saturday on the occasion of a pleasant and interesting gathering.

By invitation of the Governors many parents and students of the district inspected the school and playgrounds and subsequently assembled in the large hall which was embellished with rambler roses and various plants – where appropriate speeches where delivered.

The Rt Hon Sir John Brunner, Bart (chairman of the governors) presided and among those present were Mr H Powell (chairman of the Surrey Education Committee), the Hon Mrs Blyth, Miss Waterer, and Messrs H. Poulter, Theo Allen, T. A. Rickman J.P., R. Waterer and W. Paice, C.C(governors).

A pleasing incident marked the opening of the proceedings, as Miss Eastaugh was presented with a bouquet by a student (Miss Boullin) and Blanche Nicholson, another student, handed Mrs Powell a pretty bunch of flowers.

THE CHAIRMAN...

The Chairman, in greeting the company and bidding them welcome to the building, said he hoped that those who had seen the building and its furniture would be as pleased as he was with the result of the Governors' work. In fact as he was one of them he was quite ready to take any amount of praise which they might be pleased to bestow upon them for their success (applause). The idea which was dominating his mind was that they were present to show their devotion to a very great work, which was to bring a stimulating, elevating and ennobling influence upon all of the young people of Chertsey and a considerable area round it.

Sir John said that he had seen the students at work in the gymnasium, where his impression was that they all kept excellent time and were very graceful. He also found a number of them examining methods in which various salts could be dissolved in water, and he told them how his chemical laboratories in Cheshire were engaged in work....

THE FIRST REPORT

Miss Eastaugh then presented her report of the progress and work of the school. She said the keynote of her remarks was gratitude to the great founder of the school, to the people of the neighbourhood, to the governors for the way in which they had devoted themselves to making the buildings perfect, and to the county authorities for their support and ready help in all matters; and to Sir John Brunner without whom they could not have obtained their playing fields. Miss Eastaugh said her chief object had been to produce a course which would develop the minds and bodies of the children, and they might arrive at the best interpretation of life and be able to exercise the highest ideals of usefulness and happiness (applause). She then mentioned that the students numbered 46, and also referred to the various subjects taught. In conclusion she expressed her appreciation of the skill and enthusiasm with which her staff had taken up their work.

On the motion of Mr P Saunders, who spoke from the body of the hall, thanks were accorded to Sir John and the Governors. The senior class then nicely sang, 'Hark, the goat bells ringing' and the juniors the 'Recessional'. The proceedings terminated with the National Anthem, after which the company were provided with tea and coffee.

The celebration of the opening of the new school took place just eleven days before the outbreak of the First World War. The consequent disruption of families, movement of staff and pressure on pupils to get work rather than stay at school created unforeseen difficulties. The arrival of a team of Inspectors within the school's first year may not have been welcome at the time but their report gives a taste of school life in 1915.

REPORT OF THE UNIVERSITY OF LONDON INSPECTORS ON THE EDUCATIONAL WORK OF THE SIR WILLIAM PERKINS'S SCHOOL, CHERTSEY - MARCH 1915

Sir William Perkins's School is a secondary school for girls, intended to serve an extensive area, including Byfleet and Woking. It is not a very populous district, its development in part being hampered by a very indifferent train service. There is no other public secondary school nearer than Kingston (Tiffin Girl's School) and Guildford (County School). Many of the pupils come from a considerable distance by train or bicycle. Of those attending the school at the time of the Inspection about 40 per cent. had previously been in elementary schools, about 17 per cent. in public secondary schools, and about 30 per cent. in private schools, and the rest had been taught at home. The general level of attainment on admission, even of the older girls, is not high.

The accommodation provided is very satisfactory. On the site of the original main building of the charity school a new building has been erected which is substantial and pleasing from the architectural point of view. It contains classrooms for 150 pupils, a science laboratory, an art room, and an assembly hall (on the first floor). A separate small building in the front of the school has been suitably equipped as a gymnasium; another at the back, is used for sundry purposes: as an overflow for the bicycle shed, which is too small to accommodate all the bicycles, and as a storeroom for gardening implements, etc. It may be possible, in course of time, to utilise it for the teaching of domestic economy.

The other rooms are bright, cheerful rooms, and well furnished. The only matters to which objection could be taken are the position of the blackboards, which are too low on the wall, and the distribution of the electric light points, which is not suitable for a classroom.

There is a small fiction library in the art room; and the Chairman of the Governors has given evidence of his keen interest in the school by promising to provide a reference library.

The following table shows the number of pupils in each Form and their average age at the time of the Inspection, as well as the amount of time per week given to preparation in class and at home.

Form	No. of Pupils	Average age	Preparation In Class	At Home
IV	12	15y	45 minutes	7 hours 50
IIIA	14	14y	1 hour	7 hours 40
IIIB	21	13y	1 hour 10	6 hours 40
II	11	11y	30 minutes	5 hours

Total number of pupils 58

The distribution of periods during the day is as follows:

Morning: 9.20 – 10   10.5 – 10.45   Drill   10.45 – 11 or 11 – 11.15
             11.20 – 12   12.5 – 12.45

Afternoon: 2 – 2.45   2.45 – 3.30

This amounts to 22 hours 5 minutes per week, which includes preparation, drill and games amounting in the aggregate to about three hours, so that the actual time in which the girls receive instruction is about 19 hours per week. Owing to the train service it would be difficult to prolong the afternoon session beyond 3.30.

The curriculum appears well adapted to the needs of the girls. French is the only foreign language taught and considering the relatively short school hours it is wise not to attempt a second foreign language. Even as it is the allowance of time for some important subjects is rather scanty; thus Forms IV and IIIA hardly have enough time for English, and Form IIIB has only one period a week for History and Geography respectively. Drawing only receives a single period weekly in each Form, instead of a double period.

There was a crispness in some of the comments made by the Inspectors:

English: 'The reading aloud heard in Form IIIA was in most cases rather faint and indistinct. The Form made quite a good appearance in an attempt to classify the English consonants. A well conducted lesson was heard on the different kinds of subordinate clause but the exercises set seemed to be beyond the compass of some of the girls who are not at all clear about the functions of the different parts of speech.'

Mathematics: 'It would also add to the value and interest of the lessons in Arithmetic if the mistresses would supplement the examples in the text books by some original problems of their own, bearing upon the household and other matters which make a special appeal to girls. Too little attention is given to neatness and accuracy in geometrical constructions. Hard and well sharpened pencils should always be used for this work, which is best done on unlined paper.'

French: 'The pronunciation is not yet as good as may nowadays be expected in a secondary school for girls. The vowel sounds are often English rather than French. The teacher should often read fresh matter in the text book herself, letting the pupils repeat each breath-group after her, in chorus. Only in this way will they acquire the 'melody' of French Speech. At present their reading is faint and uninteresting.'

Geography: 'To prevent discursiveness in the lessons, to avoid waste of time and to obviate vagueness, it is imperative before the lesson to have clearly in mind the points the lesson is to bring out and the principles and facts which are to be made clear. Side issues must be avoided, desultory questions must be checked, and alert attention on the part of every girl must be expected.'

Science: 'The girls must be taught to distinguish between essential points and trivial details. Unnecessarily elaborate sketches of apparatus should be discouraged. Neatness, good arrangement, and correct spelling must be insisted upon; and altogether the girls must be taught to take a greater pride in their note-books, which must be supervised more scrupulously.'

The Inspectors report concluded with a paragraph full of compliments and encouragement. Miss Eastaugh must have glowed with pleasure as she read it.

The staff made a very favourable impression. They are thoroughly keen and very capable; and with further experience will develop into excellent teachers. They all work hard, co-operating loyally with the Headmistress, who undertakes a great deal of teaching herself. She possesses a very attractive personality and spares no pains in establishing sound traditions and in enhancing the efficiency of the school. In her endeavours she receives the wholehearted support of the Governing Body, who are fully alive to the great value of the Sir William Perkins's School for the extensive district is serves. A most promising start has been made, and all concerned have reason to anticipate an ever increasing sphere of usefulness for the work of the school.

The Foundation Secondary School for Girls Chertsey on Thames in the County of Surrey Prospectus 1918

Aim of the School

The school is intended to provide for Girls a liberal mental and physical training, which will fit them for life – domestic, professional or commercial, and make them healthy and graceful.

It is strongly advised that the girl of average ability and opportunities should follow the ordinary School course until she has passed through the Sixth Form, in which she will be prepared for the General School Examination and for the Matriculation Examination of the University of London.

Curriculum

The School Course includes: Holy Scripture; the English Language and Literature; History – English and Foreign; Geography – Local, Physical and Political; Languages – French and Latin; Mathematics – Arithmetic, Algebra and Geometry; Science –

Physics, Chemistry, Domestic Science and Gardening.
Class singing
Art: Brushwork, Model Drawing, Shading, Design.
Needlework and Elementary Dressmaking.
Physical Training: Gymnastics, Swedish Drill, Organised Games.
Arrangements can be made for private lessons on the pianoforte and violin. The fee for such tuition will be from £1 1s per term.
Dancing Classes are held in the Autumn and Spring Terms.

Admission

Application for admission must be made on a printed form to be obtained at the School, and forwarded to the Head Mistress. Pupils will be admitted at the age of eight and upwards.

It is most desirable that pupils should enter the School as early as possible so that they may receive the full advantage of a Secondary School Course.

There is an entrance examination graduated according to age, which includes as a minimum:

Reading   Writing   English Composition

Arithmetic. The first four rules simple and compound.

Sir W Perkins's School

7 free Place exam

Terms

1 How much cord would you require for the qu edges of a spout cushion 25 ins long 17 ins wide allowing 3 ins at each corner for the loops? what would it cost at 9ᵈ per yd.?

2 You can send a telegram containing 12 words for 1/0, each extra word costs ½ᵈ. Find the cost of sending this : Smith, Grasmere, Worthing. Engage four rooms all august inclusive terms wiring date and time of arrival. Briscoe

3 If the date of 6 persons were entered as July 1ˢᵗ 1886, March 10ᵗʰ 1894, May 6ᵗʰ 1841, Jan 22ⁿᵈ 1899 Feb. 10ᵗʰ 1926, Nov. 20ᵗʰ 1900, What are there ages in years & complete months today?

4 The prince of W ales made a tour of 10,000 mls in 6 mths find what his average of travel was in miles per day (4 wks in a mth)

5 War saving certificates are 15/6 each a man bough 100 in 1916 how much money will he own now if each is worth 1£ after being invested five years.

14 Entrance test for a free place at SWPS in 1928. Unfortunately no official copy of the school entrance examination from the 1920's has survived but a test paper was copied out by hand by one

Fees

The fees are as follows:

	PER TERM		
	£	s	d
For Girls residing in Chertsey, Egham, Thorpe or Chobham	2	6	8
For Girls residing within the administrative County of Surrey and not in Chertsey, Egham, Thorpe or Chobham	2	13	4
For Girls residing outside the administrative County of Surrey	3	6	8

These fees cover tuition in all the subjects of the School curriculum, and include games and the use of the stationery, text-books and scientific instruments.

Fees must be paid before the first Monday of each term and to a School Account at Barclay's Bank, Chertsey branch. The Governors reserve the right to exclude from the school, girls whose fees are not paid punctually.

Exemptions from payment of tuition fees are to an extent of not less than 5 percent of the girls admitted to the School during the previous school year, shall be offered on admission to girls resident in any one of the Parishes of Chertsey, Thorpe, Egham or Chobham, who are, and have for not less than two years, been in attendance at Public Elementary Schools.

> & owing to coal "strikes ⅓ of the trains were immidiatly cancelled - if 46 now run per day from Liverpool St to Cambridge how many ran before?
>
> English
> Write a description of a journey by one of the following a train, bicycle, char-a-banc, aroplane, yacht (this need not be true. Do you believe in fairies? tell me all about it give meaning of the following lines :— If I should die
>
> think only this of me That there's some corner of a foreign field That is for-ever England.
>
> put the following into sentences to show that you understand the meaning - census, R36, wireless, mascot, memorial If you were in a strange town with no means of getting home what would you do

candidate. Many years later she found it among her papers and sent it to the school for the archive. Recent candidates may like to decide whether the standard has become more or less difficult!

Notice of Removal

Parents or Guardians are required to give in writing to the Head Mistress at least half a term's notice of intention to remove a pupil, or in default, must pay half the term fee. The same rule applies to the discontinuing of an extra subject.

Attendance and Holidays

The school hours are from 9.30am to 1.15pm and from 2.30pm to 4pm. Saturday is a whole holiday.

Regular and punctual attendance is required.

No girl may be absent from the School without previous permission from the Head Mistress, except in case of illness, and in this case, written notice stating the nature of the illness, should be sent at once to the Head Mistress.

Hot dinners are provided for pupils wishing to dine at the School, for which a charge of 9d. is made, or £2 5s. for the term, payable in advance.

Pupils may bring cold lunch, and a charge of $1/2$ d. per day is made for use of table requisites.

During the morning girls may purchase milk at the school.

The School year is divided in to three Terms, the holidays being, approximately, three weeks at Easter, seven weeks in the summer, and three weeks at Christmas.

Physical Training

The whole School is drilled every day, and attends a gymnastic class with apparatus work once a week.

Every girl takes part in the School Games.

School Dress

Every girl is required to wear a school hat, with the School hat band.

In School hours, girls wear the School gymnastic dress, a pattern of which may be seen at the School.

The same costume and rubber soled shoes are worn for Games and Physical Training Classes.

Miscellanea

A careful record of the weight and height of each girl is kept and compared from term to term, anything abnormal being notified to the parents.

No pupil is allowed to return to School at the beginning of the Term without the School

Health Certificate signed by her parent or guardian. No pupil is allowed to return to School on recovery from infectious disease, or to attend from a house in which there is or has been, infectious disease without a medical certificate that she can do so without danger to pupils.

The Head Mistress very much hopes that parents will interview her personally and for this purpose will be at the School on Thursday afternoons during Term, between 2.30 and 4pm., or at other times by appointment.

The next term will begin on September 12th 1918

New pupils will be examined on

1918 Remembered

Miss Christine Wilcox, born in 1911, entered Form II of Sir William Perkins's School in 1918 when she was seven years old.

Miss Christine Wilcox, born in 1911, entered Form II of Sir William Perkins's School in 1918 when she was seven years old.

Miss Wilcox travelled to school by train from Addlestone to Chertsey, (in those days it was only one penny return!) Miss Wilcox and the other younger girls were met by their form teacher, Miss Derrie, at the station. Miss Derrie escorted the girls to school because even then Guildford Road was very busy, only with horses and carts, not cars and lorries!

Like today, girls were never allowed to enter the school by the main entrance but had to use a back entrance.

In 1918 the only buildings were the main school building and the old gym. Behind the school building were netball courts and an old chapel which was used as a gardeners hut. The library as we know it today used to be the assembly hall and where the dance and deportment classes were held. What is now room nine used to be the dining room and the music practice rooms were once the prefects' common rooms.

The school dinners were very good. The girls ate meals like steak pie and 'spotted dog' for pudding and there was always fish on Friday. All the dinner tables had plates of vegetables on them and the Head Mistress, Miss Eastaugh, used to eat with the girls and maybe have her main course on one table and move on to another table to eat her dessert.

In 1918, the winter uniform was a navy blue serge gym slip, a specially made white long-sleeved blouse and a navy blue tie with yellow and white stripes (like today), a navy blue blazer with the badge embroidered on the pocket and a hat to match with the badge on the front and a navy band with white and yellow stripes with a bow on the side. White gloves (just imagine it!) were worn and black shoes with calf length white socks. The summer uniform was the same but the gym-slip was made out of a stiff, silk material

15 The Staff Hockey Team 1921.

and they wore straw boaters. The teachers wore black caps and gowns all the time.

Miss Wilcox took most of the subjects that are taught today: French, English, Maths, Latin, History, Geography, General Science and Needlework. Miss Wilcox had nearly all her lessons in her form room with the exception of her General Science lesson which was held in the science lab which was in the main building (now Rooms 4 and 5). Once a week there was a 'divinity lesson', which Miss Eastaugh took. This lesson consisted of showing the girls how to cut their nails and brush their hair properly etc.

Miss Wilcox said that she was a bad pupil and that she was always playing tricks on the teachers like putting drawing pins on their chairs!

The girls also had gym lessons and judging by the size of the old gym you can imagine what a small number of pupils there were at the time! The pupils were given a green stripe to wear on their gym-slip if they passed their gym test, a red stripe if they were good all round gym , and a blue stripe if they were good at movement to music.

In the period when Miss Wilcox was at school you paid more to go to the school the further away from it you lived so you were considered lucky if you lived in Chertsey. Your parents had to be of 'independent means' to go to the school, i.e. your parents had to have their own business or inherited wealth.

Miss Wilcox remembers the 200th anniversary of the school in 1925. She says that they hardly had any lessons for two weeks and some of the senior girls dressed up in the original school uniform of 1725 and rode in a horse and cart down Guildford Road with the whole school walking behind! To mark the anniversary the school bought the field which used to stand next to the main building. This is now where the present assembly hall stands, (built in 1959).

Miss Wilcox left Sir William Perkins's in 1926 after having passed her general certificate of education and matriculated.

Miss Wilcox went on to become a nurse and was very active during the Blitz in London in the Second World War as she is a trained fire woman.

Miss Wilcox in now 77 years old, retired, and living in Addlestone where she lived when she was a child.

Interview recorded by Maureen Brophy L6A
Published in Sir William Perkins's School Magazine 1988/1989

The Bi-Centenary Celebrations : July 1925

To mark the anniversary of its foundation the school organised a number of fund raising events in order to buy the adjoining field. This corner of land where the Assembly Hall and Science Block now stands was traditionally the site for visiting fairs and the circus. Their close presence over the boundary fence was not always congenial to Miss Eastaugh. Her solution was to purchase the field.

The combined earnings from the school fete, a tennis tournament and a performance of 'The Rivals' fell short of the sum needed. Nobly, Sir Edward Stern, a governor and local landowner, came to the rescue and made up the deficit.

FROM MISS EASTAUGH'S LETTERS TO PUPILS AND OLD GIRLS IN 'THE RAMBLER'

I am sure that we are all rejoicing in our latest acquisition – which for twelve years has been my Naboth's vineyard – and now, for obvious reasons – may be called Stern Field. I quite miss the gipsies' washing, and even more – and in quite a different way – their chickens, cats and dogs and progeny, who wandered over our grounds. I hope that they are all very happy elsewhere.

You remember how I delight in new experiences – for instance – in walking down Guildford Street escorted by two policemen, as we did on our way to Church at the Bi-Centenary Celebrations – well – I did another fresh thing this week – I went to tea with an Old Girl who was married. It was a great pleasure – may I have more of the same nature? I feel that all the news must be told in the magazine, but if you feel that there is anything further you want to know – come along and see us. There is tea in my room at four o'clock – nearly always!

My love to you,

M.A.E   (1926)

As I write I can see some girls playing on the hard court in summer dresses, which are more or less an innovation – and look so attractive when put on properly. I feel that the day is coming when I must seriously consider light stockings – if I can find some way of avoiding the pink tints, which are so ugly and prevalent.

All the girls wore beaver coloured stockings on our trip to Provence   (1931)

This summer we have had new summer frocks of blue gingham – made to our own design, smartly cut and buttons down the front. I think that all would approve of them.

I sometimes wish that there was more time to discuss things like dress with you – as I am sure that it is a subject in which valuable instruction could be given.
Probably you remember the one thing I do believe and try to impress on you is that it is your every-day working outfit which should cost most as it has to stand the hardest wear, and it is the people who see you everyday who are either pleased or pained by your appearance. Possibly you may think this is a strange letter for a Headmistress to write for the magazine – it simply means that I want the best possible for you always – and as I know that fundamentally you are all dears and well worth knowing – I want you to appear your attractive selves at all times.   (1937)

16 The Bi-Centenary Celebrations for July 22 1925. Front and back cover of the programme.

17 Dorothy Geraldine Taylor in her new school uniform 1927.

18 Girls wearing winter and summer uniform about 1929. Lilian Gosden, Lavinia Hunt, Daisy Pearce and Winifred Ottaway.

19 Miss Eastaugh and Form Va visit Mr Tulk's former college at Oxford in 1938.

20 SWPS party holding up the traffic on their way to a West End production – The Rambler 1933.

21 The expedition to Oxford – The Rambler.

The School during the War

Mrs Jean Austin (née Ward), a pupil from 1938 – 1946

I attended Sir William Perkins's School from September 1938 to July 1946, during Miss Eastaugh's headship. Due to the war commencing in 1939 the staff did not change much and I remember Miss Davey (Deputy Head and History), Miss Duncan (Science) Mrs White (English) Miss Williams (French), Miss Jackman (Maths) Miss Hoad (Art), Miss Goddard (Geography), Miss Kemp (Latin) and Miss Derry (Needlework). I especially remember Miss Goddard's beautiful maps to be found on blackboards in every classroom.

The grounds, formal gardens in front and grass hockey pitches behind the school, were kept up by a groundsman called "West", who spent much of his time on the 'ride-on mower', which was quite a novelty then. There were only three buildings. The main school, a small building across a netball court called the library, but which had originally held a small Lower School, and the gymnasium, which was very modern for those days. Four large air-raid shelters were added to the right of the main building in 1939.

Many girls came by train or bus from Walton, Hersham, Weybridge, Byfleet, Addlestone, Ottershaw and Egham. Very few of the pupils were actually from Chertsey and these either cycled or walked. As I remember, my parents paid three guineas a term tuition fees as did the Egham girls. There was a reciprocal arrangement for Chertsey boys attending Strodes School in Egham. Other Surrey girls paid seven guineas and girls from out of the County paid ten guineas a term.

When I first attended the school we wore navy gym slips with white blouses, the School tie of blue with gold stripes and black stockings and shoes. We wore navy blazers or navy gabardine raincoats with navy velour hats having bright yellow bands. Summer frocks were blue check and it was compulsory to wear knickers to match and we wore Panama hats with yellow bands. In summer white 'lisle' stockings were worn unless the pupil was in the third form or under a certain height, when white ankle socks were allowed. We were always expected to wear white gloves, light ones in summer, which were not practical on a bicycle, especially as I often had to carry my cycle up over the pedestrian bridge of the railway for fear of being late. We also had to have indoor shoes as well as outdoor shoes. For Speech Day in July we were expected to wear white dresses with white knickers, (and a member of staff inspected our knickers to make sure we were correctly dressed). We were also expected to obtain a Dorothy Perkins rose. With the coming of the war many of these clothes were abandoned. The white dress made by my mother with tucks and hems to allow for growth in future years was not needed again and we soon gave up hats, lisle stockings and summer gloves.

When the war started we went to school in shifts as the shelters were not built. We all

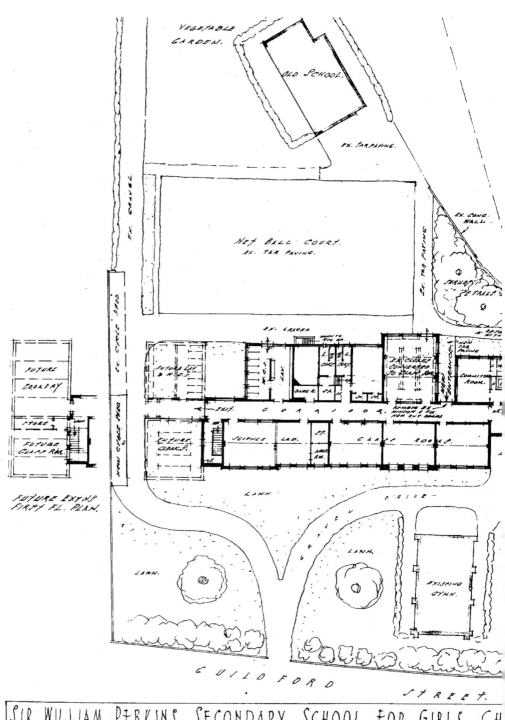

VEGETABLE GARDEN.

OLD SCHOOL.

EX. TAR PAVING.

EX. CONC. WALL

NET BALL COURT.
EX. TAR PAVING.

EX. TAR PAVING.

SHRUBS & TREES.

EX. GRAVEL.

EX. GRAVEL.

NEW CYCLE SHED

EX. CYCLE SHED

FUTURE COOKERY

FUTURE LAV. & W.C.S.

FUTURE STORE

FUTURE CLOAK RM.

FUTURE CLOAK RM.

SCIENCE LAB.

CLASS ROOMS.

COMMITTEE ROOM.

FUTURE EXT'N.P FIRST FL. PLAN.

LAWN.

LAWN.

LAWN.

LAWN.

GRAVEL DRIVE

EXISTING GYMN.

GUILDFORD STREET.

SIR WILLIAM PERKINS SECONDARY SCHOOL FOR GIRLS, CH
PROPOSED NEW CLOAKROOM BLOCK (NASHCRETE HUT) & CONV

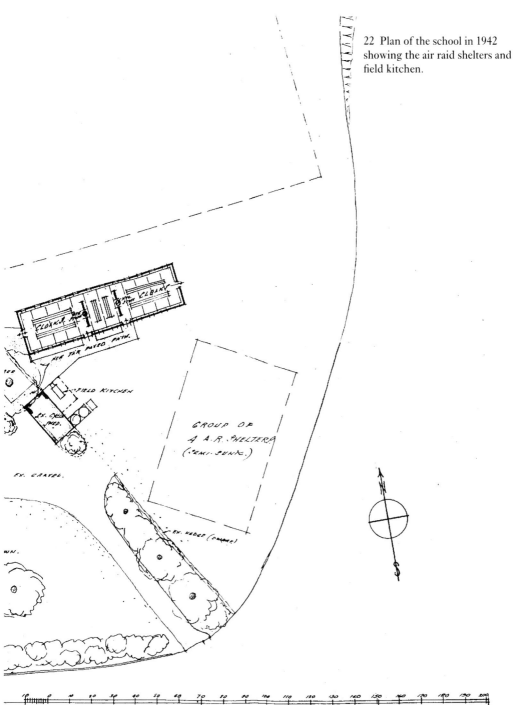

22 Plan of the school in 1942 showing the air raid shelters and field kitchen.

CLOAKR

STO CLOAK.

HOR TAR PAVED PATH.

FIELD KITCHEN

EX. CHES. SHED.

GROUP OF
4 A.R. SHELTERS
(SEMI-SUNK.)

EX. GRAVEL.

EX. HEDGE (GARDEN)

N

S

Y. SKETCH PLAN. SCALE: 20 FEET TO 1 INCH
OF EXISTING CLOAKROOM FOR USE AS CLASSROOM.

JARVIS & RICHARDS, ARCHS.
1, SPEDDING ST. SLOANE SQ.
DEC. 1942.   S.W.1.

had to be able to line up in the lower corridor away from danger of flying glass, which reduced the numbers allowed to be in the building. The first term was chaotic as girls came and went as people moved around the country finding 'safe' places in which to live. When we did attend school there were always new girls in the classroom – many only stayed a short time. Gradually things settled. My year officially commenced in 1939. I remained in the third form for two years as I was very young, having gone to the school when I was only ten years old. This year was the first to have a two form entry. There were about twenty five girls in each class and we were two parallel classes split alphabetically and called 3P and 3L, being the first and last letters of the word parallel.

During the second year of the war St. Olaves and St. Saviours Girls' Grammar School were evacuated to Chertsey and they needed to use our Science lab, gymnasium and games facilities, so many of our classes were held in the Abbey Barn, a beautiful old building at the other end of the town. The school day was cut short as the train and the bus girls were given time to walk there and back at the end of the day. Later the London school took over Pyrcroft House and gave up using our facilities. When the evacuees finally returned to London, Sir William Perkins's School took over Pyrcroft House. The school was expanding, particularly after the 1944 Education Act. All the third forms, (first years) were based at Pyrcroft. As a sixth former and prefect I remember walking the crocodiles of little girls up to Pyrcroft. We also had to go and take them on a bus to the Masonic Hall for dinner as the school had outgrown its kitchen and dining room.

Many sixth form lessons took place at Pyrcroft when staff were time-tabled there. I seemed to spend so much of my school life walking or cycling from building to building.

During 1940 to 1942 lessons were often delayed as staff and pupils would arrive late due to trains not running as the lines had been bombed during the night. Many of us had to spend sleepless nights and it was not unusual for staff to tell us to lay our heads on our hands on our desks and try to sleep, as we were all too tired to concentrate. In those days we remained in our form room for most lessons and the staff moved round to us. My year did all our School Certificate Examinations in the shelters. The rest of the school remained at home so the staff could give their attention to us and because there was no room in the shelters as our desks were spread out in them. This was the period of the flying bombs.

There were no school outings during the war. Miss Goddard described exciting trips which had taken place to Paris prior to the war. Soon after the war was over Miss Goddard arranged an outing to Leith Hill to help us understand physical geography. It was a great adventure for us. Flo as she was affectionately called, was, in my opinion, one of the best teachers. I learnt much from her, including a love of reading, not inspired by the English staff.

During my fifth form days a School Council was formed of staff and pupils and the pupil representatives managed to get Miss Eastaugh's agreement to split the school into houses for sports and other competitions. Previously sports competitions had been inter-form. The houses were given the names of past and present Chairman of Governors. John Tulk was Chairman throughout the war. He was a collector of fine pieces of furniture and his house was a veritable museum. Before the war he always gave leavers a Tennis Party. This was a great day out, with special food sent up to his house from the school kitchens. These tennis parties continued, I think, for some time until there was no longer a gardener to keep the grass courts in good order. My year, having missed out on this, was invited to a viewing of his precious collection, (much of which was already catalogued by the British Museum). As he always gave prizes for the tennis parties he decided to give a present to one of us. I drew the piece of paper with a cross on it and still treasure the delicate glass cake stand which I was given. I was not allowed to take it home on my cycle. I had to walk to Miss Eastaugh's house in the evening to collect my prize which was in a box all wrapped up in a pair of Mr Tulk's old pyjamas!

I left school as Miss Eastaugh retired and my final memory is of her leaving party with Governors and Staff when the sixth form entertained them with a Minstrel Show.

Mrs Eileen Biddle (née Clarke) a pupil from 1941 –1946

Our life style was drastically changed by the advent of war. Food rationing obviously had its effect on school meals. Hot dinners were provided for which a charge of one shilling was made daily. I don't know how the school managed with the rationing but I do remember a particularly horrid pudding, said to be ' a trifle', made of cubes of bread dunked in a watery custard with a small dollop of marrow and ginger jam. Other delicacies were whale meat, a fish called Snoek, rice pudding or tapioca made with water and no sugar – all featured at least once a week on the school menu.

The school uniform was kept for as long as possible but as one grew out of an article of clothing the replacements were different. Gym slips were not pleated as before, less material being used. Blouses became square necked with no tie. In summer, the school gingham dress was allowed to be home made in any reasonable style provided it was check and in your house colour: green, blue, red or yellow.

A total of 66 clothing coupons had to last a year. A school blazer was 8 coupons, a shirt 3 coupons, a yard of cloth required 3 coupons and so on. Credit is certainly due to our mothers who still managed to keep us smart as the school's high standards were still insisted upon.

Long hair would not have been seen in my day. Hair was not allowed to touch the collar though pigtails were permitted. Nails and necks were inspected regularly. I remember one teacher asked me if my hair was permed. 'No', was my answer. 'it is naturally curly.' She still marched me to the wash basin to check for herself!

Large school satchels were needed as we had an enormous amount of homework, three subjects most evening and five at the weekend. Many a tearful evening was spent begging my father to help me with Algebra only to find he'd got it wrong as well when the homework was returned.

Air raids were a problem, though nothing on the scale of the London Bombings. The railways were always a target and many German Bombers jettisoned their bombs before or after their main targets if the anti-aircraft were more active. We had air raid drills, practice and real, and most of the children, like me were more than pleased if the sirens went off in the middle of a Maths lesson. The most unpopular teachers were those who endeavoured to continue their lesson in the shelter. The journeys by train to and from school were often disrupted due to debris on the lines, de-railments and diversions but I don't remember it being too difficult. I seem to remember that part of the school grounds were used for growing vegetables. 'Dig for Victory' was the call of the day.

However life at school was kept as normal as possible. Miss Eastaugh, the Head Mistress, was unforgettable. To be summoned to her study was guaranteed to bring the most rebellious child to heel. I recall on one occasion I was blowing my nose in the corridor. Observed by her I was beckoned into her study and given a lecture on the etiquette of nose-blowing. 'Young ladies never, but never, use two hands' she said. 'One hand is quite sufficient; it is not a meal.'

Miss Eastaugh's words to the new girls at the beginning of the autumn term were

'I hope that you will have a happy and successful school career but you must remember this. You will do as you are told when you are told. Have I made myself clear?'

CHAPTER SIX

Sir William Perkins's Voluntary Controlled Grammar School for Girls 1946

The Butler Education Act of 1944 ushered in a new national policy on secondary schooling and when in 1946 Miss Margaret Sames took up her appointment it was as Head of a Voluntary Controlled Grammar School run by Surrey County Council. Now girls were awarded places on the result of the Surrey 11+ examination and fee paying came to an end. It was to be a time of growth and improved academic standards.

Miss Sames recalled some of her experiences in two articles she wrote for the 1975 edition of 'The Rambler'.

When Miss Sames was appointed in 1946 the war was over but there was still rationing of clothes and food. The air-raid shelters where even public examinations had been conducted on horrid slatted forms for seats remained until 1959. The brick soup kitchen in the garden by the Headmistress' study bred mosquitoes and smelt insanitary. It was pronounced sacred because it was War Department Property and no-one would move it officially. One summer evening the Headmistress and gardener armed with sledge hammer and pick-axe, enacted a scene from Holy Scriptures and walked Joshua wise, seven times round the walls. Next day the relics were removed and the War Department never knew.

Where is now the library was the hall; it was thrown into room 9 when the school assembled for lunch, which in those days was mince, mince and still more mince. There was a hatch in the adjoining careers room but which was then the kitchen – and which housed an old coal kitchen range which smoked so appallingly in the early morning that the cooks fled into the corridor and prayers were conducted in a sooty, choking murk. One week-end the range was replaced by gas stoves and thereafter we managed to keep some kitchen staff.

In 1946 the school council was established though it did not get its first written constitution for several years. The standard of debate varied from the cogent and witty to the flaccid and inane, which is one illustration of the fact that the school is a microcosm of the macrocosm. Very many sensible suggestions were promptly implemented. In the same year the first Careers Mistress was appointed; the school charity was instituted and for long played an important role in school life. Not long after an 'internal certificate' was established to encourage those who at the end of their fifth year were not in all ways as capable as their friends; this was before the days of the CSE and the studies were examined traditionally, but it was nonetheless forward looking.

From 1945 to 1960 pupils in the first two years spent their mornings at Pyrcroft House and their afternoons in the Main School. On Friday mornings all, by praying together, felt a united whole.

Numbers grew largely because the Sixth Form gradually increased fifteen fold. In 1956 pressure on space was slightly eased by the building of the Domestic Science or Home Economic Unit and because the Gardener, the Caretaker and Headmistress converted the Staff Bicycle shed into a coaching room; this happily forced authority to provide it with heating, lighting and flooring. It was a charming though short lived room, bulldozed in 1959 to make space for the covered way.

In 1960 the new wing was built after a great deal of trouble and discussion. The Governors finally managed to circumvent those who wished to build an electric sub-station facing the front door, or failing that, under the new hall windows. The old hall was saved from being carved up into three classrooms and was made into a library. At last it was possible to teach Physics and Chemistry and the Biological Sciences as separate studies and in a reasonable way.

In 1961 new hard tennis courts were laid down in the field beyond the stream. Ever since 1948 the Headmistress had been agitating for more playing fields. By 1964 there was talk of its coming. In 1964, the year of our Jubilee Celebrations, the school launched its Pavilion Fund and with financial assistance and guidance of the Trustees and with devoted technical assistance from one Governor, Mr Herd, and with helpful efforts of many people the Pavilion was available for use in 1967 when the new field was also ready.

Long before 1960 the Governors, looking to that time when generations of children would no longer have the wildness of Pyrcroft Garden, tried to buy the triangle of railway land along the track. Ultimately the Wilderness was purchased and planted with shrubby trees, which will perhaps grow one day into bosky woods. Trees, bushes, shrubs, flowers over the years have been given and planted by innumerable friends.

It would take a chapter to describe these, from the plum for which a post-war cook had 60lbs of extra sugar ration for jam making up to those planted in memory of Miss Eastaugh.

In 1964 the shell of the staff room and the cloakroom were built and thanks to the great generosity of a few parents they were finished in a really civilised way.

The real substance of any community is made not of the buildings but of the people, the pupils, teachers and governors. They cannot adequately be dealt with in a few notes, not even in a chapter; it would be invidious to pick out individuals. However, as we began with Sir William we ought to close with John Tulk, benefactor to the whole town, by whose will the school, in 1956 received money and treasures.

PYRCROFT 1945 – 1960

'The falling house that never falls', that was how, in 1948, I referred to Rupert Brooke's nostalgic words, to that much loved building already mellowed by some 200 years. The name indeed was much older for the terrain is quoted in a document of Henry 11's reign as Pyr croft, the pear orchard.

In 1946 when I first knew the place it was a headmistress's nightmare. It was inconvenient, the Cinderella part of the school on a split site, with seven plumbing systems, trailing fraying electric wiring, open coal fires, with only four lavatories, one for the staff, two outside for the 120 girls and one indoors which the resident staff kindly allowed one form to use; with one kitchen range on which to cook 125 lunches daily. Today in 1975, no domestic staff would come, no teaching staff would stay and pupil power would 'demonstrate' in cunning and devious ways.

23 Pyrcroft House in 1947.

And yet, and yet and yet… How is it possible to estimate the benefits that accrued from having to make virtues out of necessities? How to explain the intimacy and the warmth, the fun and graciousness, the kindly benevolence that the old house and above all its garden gave to fifteen generations of Perkins's girls? Perhaps the only way will be to jog the memories of those happy ones who were fortunate to pass their mornings in such an unofficial setting.

On May 27th 1960 the removals men arrived; and as they loaded their goods (ancient, mostly oak, desks with fixed seats) the children ate a last picnic lunch and on the lawn gathered informally with teachers, cook, the gardener and the domestic staff for a last brief service of thanksgiving and for prayers that future generations of children at school on the site would be as happy as we had been, and would, in spite of alterations, capture something of its charm. There was a last cheer for the old house, one last visit to the 'camps' in the copses as the removals men fetched the last load. A couple of individuals scurried around the building kissing the bricks until they were scooped up by form mistresses. Mrs Showell and I drank a last cup of tea at a desk too old to be moved, and looked out of the beautifully proportioned window, shook our heads at a forgotten satchel (no briefcases in those days) abandoned on the grass. We picked it up; then we too left the place.

And now to jog the thoughts of some of you. Do you remember the nest with the fledglings in the old pump, the soft plop of over ripe green figs that dropped on a summers day from the immense tree outside the room with the fire escape. The perfume of red may, wisteria and laburnum all holding up that lean grey stone wall, the heady scent of the huge mock orange that made concentration in the garden room difficult, the tangy smell of clipped box hedges in the formal garden? Can you recall 'lilac square' with its heavy blossom of incense where there was a perfect setting for many performances of 'A Midsummer Night's Dream'? Can you recollect the mulberry tree in the far corner, planted, the legend said, along with many others in the district in the late seventeenth century to provide silkworm cocoons for exiled Huguenot weavers? The tree grew near the Jungle Gym about which 'authority' knew nothing officially but which spread out shiny branches worn satin smooth and silver grey by endless school tunics. Only a few will remember 'the secret lily pool' but those few were very angry and sad when it was part of the garden built over by the new housing estate in 1948; but many will remember how the first crocus to come out around the oak tree was by tradition held to begin the Perkins' Spring; and all will surely remember those 'camps' in the hazel copses, furnished with stones, old bicycle wheels, plaited leaves, name plates and all the paraphernalia of imaginative childhood growing into adolescence; some were garnished, swept and tidy, others a riot of inventiveness, all were jealously guarded.

I wonder if any recall strange English lessons, politely labeled 'peripheral studies' by Her Majesty's Inspectors, when we all lay or sat on the grass all our five senses were alive as we looked, touched, listened, and smelt, and after the twig, leaf or flower had been pronounced non-poisonous, tasted. In this lazy, dozy way we acquired vast stores of synonyms, antonyms, similes and metaphors. In more business like mood we inspected the form gardens and wrote, for homework, direct and factual accounts of these before Mrs White judged them.

Which second year was it who made a baby fortune selling her form's lettuces and spring onions to the staff?

Indoors it was often hideously difficult to teach; there were no fixed blackboards, no visual aids, no 'hardware', never sufficient space even to pose an easel and balance a blackboard; dinners were eaten in form rooms on desks covered with little squares of American cloth; fire broke out in the garden room, the garden room ceiling fell on a French lesson; during the great freeze Miss Williams boiled kettles and poured the water down the lavatories and Mrs White spend her free periods in the loft heating the water tank with a hair dryer.

And yet, and yet… because of difficulties table manners were better than I ever knew them before or since; people had to be more tolerant and kindly; imagination was given a chance. If inside it was squashed, cosy and a ghastly fire risk, outside was room for games, for adventure, for secrecy, there was even a stream, forbidden territory of course, but splendid for dreaming by. If it was easy to teach about Wall 'with hair and lime knit up in thee' because one had to pluck out a bit of lime and horse hair from the hole made by too energetic pushing of that easel, it was also easy to post letters, stuck up with sealing wax into the gaping wainscot for future generations to find.

My own memories are legion, the most outstanding is a composite one covering those many lessons that I learned from the experience of organising and running a school that lived in two such buildings as we had.

As a tail piece I will mention only three more; the blue bottled side of bacon I was fetched to examine by a posse of eleven year olds. It had been tossed over the wall near the Jungle Gym by, presumably, hard pressed black marketeers, and to severely meat rationed children and to me it was a sad, and incongruous sight; the Madrigals sung from the roof in the dusk of the warm June night on the Pyrcroft Pilgrimage; and my first sight of all. It was, as I discovered later, our dear old cleaner, wearing a beret and apron, kneeling beside her zinc, pail, yellow bar soap and immense floor cloth slowly massaging with her scrubbing brush the white floor boards and moaning 'Rock of Ages mm mh mh', perhaps she was really invoking that blessing that I think, in retrospect, we can all feel.

24 Mock Election 1950

25 The Prefects' breakfast party
1951. Ann Pearce, Judith Brown,
Pat Harper, Erica Stoyles, Jill
Batley and Doreen Mcleod.

26 (*top*) The main entrance and bicycle shed 1946.
27 (*above*) The gymnasium 1962.

28 The Prefects 1954.

29 Miss Sames with the Prefects 1967.

Memories of Sir William Perkins's Grammar School 1956 – 1963

Written by Heather Williams with contributions from Anne Kingston, Gillian Townsend, Lorna Rode, Ailsa Provo, Elaine Jeffries, Heather Parish, Margaret Bromley, Glynne Simpkins, Janet Vincent.

We were the fortunate ones for we spent our first two years of secondary education at Pyrcroft which was a ten minute walk away from the main school. Nestled beneath St Ann's Hill, Pyrcroft House, part of which dates back to Elizabethan times, was an exciting place for 11 – 13 year olds though the cramped rooms and uneven floor and staircase must have been a trial to our teachers. It is said that Pyrcroft House was in Dickens's mind when he wrote Oliver Twist and that Oliver climbed through the barred window at the bottom of the main staircase. Unlike Oliver we always had plenty to eat and were made welcome by 'Cookie' who used to hand out little tastes of the lunch time menu for our approval – everyone's favourite was chocolate popcorn cut into generous slabs. There was no dining hall and we ate our dinner in our classrooms. We kept oilskin mats in our desks which we were meant to wipe after our dinner but nevertheless the odour of boiled cabbage often lingered throughout afternoon lessons.

Breaktimes were magical because there were so many places to wander – the formal gardens near the house, the 'paddock' with the remains of a pavilion, and the 'gym' at the far edge with ancient yew trees just right for swinging and climbing. There were clumps of brilliant coloured rhododendrons, a magnificent cedar and many other trees and bushes in which we made 'camps' where we played happily in our first year then handed over to the new girls as we became too old for such things.

We resented the breaks that were taken up walking to the main school for afternoon lessons. The teachers would also travel between the two schools and woe betide us if we were seen not wearing our hats! These were a curious cross between a beret and a pillbox and had whalebone inside the rim to keep them stiff. In the summer we were allowed to wear straw boaters instead. We had to wear our summer dresses on the first day of the summer term whatever the weather. Summertime also meant that the buildings were unheated. The most hated item of clothing was our navy blue knickers which to our great embarrassment we had to wear on the sports field if we forgot our shorts.

Games lessons usually began with a run round the cinder track, part of which ran parallel to the railway line much to the delight of the train drivers who used to slow down and hoot as we lumbered past. We did gym, hockey, and netball in winter and cricket, rounders, tennis and athletics in summer with matches, both home and away, held on Saturday mornings. Sports played a big part in the Group (house) system and there were inter-group matches in which everyone participated at the end of each term. At the end of the Christmas term each of the four groups (Brunner, Rollit, Rickman and Tulk) held a party in the school hall. In those days it was unusual to return to school in the evening and a lot of trouble was taken to make the parties fun with a variety of games and dances. The teachers and the tall girls usually took the part of men in the dances.

It was not until the 1960's that any social events were organised with Strodes our "brother" school in Egham although there was a considerable amount of socialising on the train to and from school! In the summer term of our first year we were taken by coach each week to Ottershaw Boys School because they had an indoor swimming pool. However the boys were kept well hidden until one thrilling occasion when the authorities had forgotten we were coming and we tramped in to the changing rooms to find it full of half naked boys!

Like most other schools at that time we managed without boys and put on a wide variety of productions including A Midsummer-Night's Dream, The Insect Play, Tartuffe, The Beggars Opera and two Gilbert and Sullivan operettas. We even did some smaller performances in Latin. We also organised talent shows often in aid of our form charities. Each form chose a different charity each term and we organised fund-raising events in the lunch hour or occasionally after school. We had a variety of school clubs that met after school with interesting speakers such as Miss Mount and Miss Littleboy at Classics Club, a missionary and various campaigners for CEWC (Council of Education for World Citizenship). School Council with two representatives from each form plus Miss Sames and two staff representatives was a forum for debate and taught us the formalities and courtesies of meetings and respect for other people's views. We also had a School Service Squad which was responsible for odd jobs such as putting linseed oil on the benches and cleaning the brass name plate at the front of the school.

Although it is not the purpose of this piece to mention individual teachers one cannot write about this era without mention of Miss Sames. Her erect bearing, silver grey hair, swept into a chignon and direct blue eyes made her an awesome figure to both pupils and young teachers. Prefects had the duty of robing her for Prayers which involved shaking her fading Oxford gown and draping it correctly around her shoulders. In winter she would have a fire burning in the fireplace in her study. Her chair would be turned side on so that her elbow rested on her desk and she would lean back in her chair with her legs crossed as she talked – often with a cigarette hanging off her lower lip. This would remain in place even when she as addressing a class of sixth formers who crowded onto the floor of her study once a week for a "current affairs" lesson. Among other things we discussed the furore over John Robinson's "Honest to God" and C P Snow's "The Two Cultures". Sometimes we glimpsed a more personal side of our Headmistress when she spoke of the problems for educated women between the Wars and also her famous relatives – Jack Warner the star of BBC 1's Dixon of Dock Green and Gert and Daisy Walter's the 1950's radio stars.

Margaret Sames was passionate about education and she worked hard to improve the facilities. She saved the old hall as a single architectural unit by turning it into the library and she oversaw the building of the domestic science unit and two new science labs. This resulted in improvements in the teaching of all sciences. "A" level zoology students were encouraged to practise their dissection techniques but ran into a problem when the manager of the local pet shop discovered what was happening to the small mammals he was regularly selling to the charming young student from Perkins!

By the beginning of the 1960's horizons were broadening and school trips were becoming the norm. In November 1961 Surrey County Council organised an educational cruise to Madeira, Tenerife and Lisbon at the subsidised cost of £17. Not surprisingly the trip was over subscribed and it was decided to allocate places to all sixth form geographers plus a few fourth years chosen by ballot. We sailed on the MS Dunera which had been built in 1937 as a troop ship. Two days battling through a force 8 gale in the Bay of Biscay were forgotten when Madeira appeared on the horizon. For the majority of us this was our first taste of Abroad and it was fabulous. Coaches took us around the island and we saw bananas, bougainvillea and fairy-tale white houses with red roofs before returning to Funchal where we had some free time to wander through the narrow streets. During the days on board our teachers and crew gave us lessons and talks. One passenger was making a radio programme for the BBC about young people's attitudes to social issues and some of us were invited to take part covering a variety of topics including the abolition of capital punishment.

These were the days when the only compulsory subject on the curriculum was R E, when the school awarded prizes for achieving 6 "O"levels and only about 50% of grammar school pupils went into the sixth form. It is good to celebrate the achievements of 40 years ago but educationalists and advisors should be aware of nostalgia when making decisions about how schools should operate today. As our school motto says we should all move forward A Spe in Spem.

30 Aerial view in 1977 showing the 1893 Infants' School, Domestic Science rooms and six chalets. The donkey field can be seen on the other side of Guildford Road.

CHAPTER SEVEN

Independent School 1978

Dr Bradburn Looks Back & Forward

Dr Bradburn wrote this article for the school magazine in 1991 when she retired from the Board of Governors after forty years service to the school.

I joined the staff of the Mathematics Department at Royal Holloway College in 1945 and a few years later the Principal, Dr Edith Batho, told me that the University of London had asked her to nominate someone to represent the University on the Governing Body of Sir William Perkins's School, a grammar school for girls in Chertsey. She wondered if I would be interested. I had no idea what Governors did except sit on the platform at Speech Days, but at that time Royal Holloway College took only women undergraduates, and since these were recruited from grammar schools, it seemed a good plan to learn something about how such schools were organised and managed, and I agreed.

I am rather hazy about those early years of my association with the school. Miss Sames was the headmistress, Mr Tulk, the Chairman of the Governors and Mr Haig-Brown the Clerk. The other Governors were local landed gentry or were people of importance in the life of Chertsey. It was all very cosy and friendly and most of the Governors were passionately involved in the welfare of a school founded 200 years earlier. It is well known that when Mr Tulk died, he bequeathed some of his valuable antiques to the Educational Foundation. At a different level another governor was able to help out with vegetables from his estate for school meals, when, in the six years after the war, food was still rationed. Another effect of the war was that paper was scarce and could not be used unnecessarily. It was before the day of the Gestetner, which enable multiple copies of documents to be made, and certainly before photocopiers, which now produce any number of instant copies of anything. The minutes of the meetings were recorded in long-hand by Mr Haig-Brown, and read aloud at the next meeting. This old system ensured that minutes were concise.

It is hard now to picture the running of the school in the 40's and 50's. it operated on a split site with the lower forms housed in Pyrcroft, an old house with lovely grounds near the foot of St Ann's Hill. It was delightful for the youngsters to have the grounds to play in with secret corners where they could invent their own activities. The forms occupied the old buildings in the Guildford Road site with a small playing field behind. The

31 Aerial view of the school in 1988. The Infants' School and one chalet are now surrounded by the Brunner, Tulk, Eastaugh Buildings and sports hall. The staff room has been extended and Domestic Science rooms have been converted to sixth form common rooms.

School Hall was what is now the library and it could only take half the school. Events like Speech Day were held in two parts, one for the Upper School and one for the Juniors. The staff had to divide their time between the sites and the timetable needed careful planning as motor cars were almost unknown and staff were dependent on bicycles or Shanks Pony.

It was inevitable that the old order changed and by the 1950's the meetings of the Governors were serviced by the Education Officer for the area and everyone was subject to much greater control by the bureaucracy of County Hall. Mr Anderson and Mr Elsworthy did a lot for the school. We acquired some new buildings, though decisions about development went through so many committees that delay seemed routine. Still the new hall was built and extra playing fields acquired and a rash of temporary classrooms made it possible to concentrate the school on one site. There were always shadows in the background. There were battles to be fought over the nature of the School and the Governors were at odds with the official County line.

I found this episode quite distasteful. The County Officials treated a deputation of Governors as if we were dirt and ignorant of educational theory and practice.

The dawn broke in the 1970's when the County cast the school aside and enabled the Governors to build literally a new school on the old foundations. Now it is served by a team with the philosophy of those I first knew, but with the drive and initiative of the early pioneers, and a Clerk who can translate their wishes into immediate action.

Throughout my association with Sir William Perkins's School , I have been impressed with the objects of helping girls to develop as individuals, of cultivating creative and practical skills and of gaining necessary qualifications to launch into a career. These traditions were maintained by the successive headmistresses, Miss Sames, Miss Timbrell and Mrs Darlow.

At recent Governors' meetings we have listened to accounts from Heads of Department of how in their subject areas they are adapting to the new style of examination, which is replacing the old Ordinary Levels. When I first joined the Governors the teachers in the school were facing similar problems.

A long established examination system consisting of school certificate and Higher School Certificate had been superceded by the new system of Ordinary and Advanced levels of GCE. These were intended to liberate schools from the restrictions of the former examinations. A School Certificate was only given to a candidate who passed in a group of subjects which had to include what are now termed core subjects. The Higher School Certificate, intended for VI formers, consisted of papers at two distinct levels, Principal and Subsidiary. Now the modern talk is of A levels and AS levels. The papers were graded Distinction, Good, Credit, and Pass. The top grade was very rare. This new liberal examination introduced over forty years ago was intended to allow pupils to take as many or as few subjects as they liked. The intention was that it freed schools from the examination pressures of the Fifth Form and Upper Sixth. There was a pious hope that pupils intending to study a subject in the VI th would not bother with the O level examination, but would only be examined in subjects about to be dropped. The ideal did not survive long as pupils, parents and teachers wanted the assurance of success in a public examination before embarking on VI th form work. Looking back, there must be a forty year cycle in the philosophy of examinations. Schools spend about ten years getting used to a system and adapting it to their needs, then it runs happily for a long period until the desire for change strikes and something 'new' is invented.

Now I am pleased that in severing my formal links with the school, I can look at all the wonderful new classrooms, laboratories and recreational areas and yet be conscious that all that is good in the educational ethos of the school flourishes, boding well for the twenty-first century.

The Responsibility of Deciding What to Do!

Lt Col Jarvis has a very long association with Sir William Perkins's School. He was Chairman of the Governors from 1982 until 1990.

During its time as a "Voluntary-Controlled" school Sir William Perkins's was maintained and run by Surrey County Council: all the teaching, all the staff appointments, building repairs and selection for entry were their responsibility. But the "Educational Foundation" – a permanent charity – still existed, retaining ownership of the land and buildings, as well as the house in Chertsey, and some small investments. During their time in charge the County Council built the school hall and some more laboratories which, being in permanent construction, became the property of the foundation – a fair deal considering the premises were being provided free of charge.

The school governors were similar to those in county grammar schools except for a few specially appointed from outside institutions like London University, the Guildford Diocese and the foundation itself. The rest were nominated by the local authorities. So the governing body comprised a wide range of character and ability ranging from a member of Royal Holloway College and the brilliant lady mathematician who did the calculations for Barnes Wallis and his bouncing bomb to one or two local shop stewards and council representatives. All, however, were proud to be governors or Sir William Perkins's School and it was hard for any newcomers on the local council, whatever their credentials, to get a place. As with all county schools at that time the governors had little power: finance was never mentioned and staffing was a matter for the County Council based on its points system. The governors occupied themselves mainly with questions like whether the National Anthem should be sung on Speech Day!

The decision to end selection in Surrey should have been foreseen. Excellent though the grammar schools were, the system of choosing three or four girls in a middle school to go to them, while so many able pupils just below that standard believed themselves to be a "failure" could no longer be supported. At the same time the number of children approaching secondary school age was falling – there were too many schools – so there was little or no chance of Sir William Perkins's School continuing to be maintained in some other form. One suggestion of forming a split site comprehensive with a school a mile away was not considered seriously. It would have meant the end of both within a few years.

When the change to comprehensive secondary education was finally announced the governors were faced with the enormous responsibility of deciding what to do. At the worst the school would close with its assets being taken over by the Charity Commission but the feeling was that somehow a girls' school on its own in a good part of Surrey with a railway station just across the road should succeed. The problem was how to set it up and find the staff. The matter was resolved when the Headmistress reported that every teacher had declared that she would stay on if the school went independent. With that wonderful encouragement the governors decided immediately to go ahead and start discussions on the changeover. In short the County Council agreed to pay for the "11 plus" girls to stay at the school until they finished (at a fee determined by them), to sell the hutted classrooms (euphemistically called "chalets") to the school and, in the interests of the school, to lease the playing fields which they had acquired by compulsory purchase and could not sell to a third party.

A revised constitution was drawn up by the Charity Commission, a new board of governors appointed and preparations made for the school to administer itself. This took longer than expected – finding a first-class Bursar and building a bungalow for the caretaker, for example, took some time. When the County Council asked for the hand over to be put back a year, the governors were only too pleased to agree. But the dealings with the Education Department did not run smooth. As the last moment they disclosed that in agreeing for the girls to stay on they meant only up to the statutory leaving age of 16 but, as a concession, they would allow the girls in the lower sixth to complete their 'A' level course.

This was an enormous blow because many parents obviously could not afford the fees, and the number registering for the sixth form fell accordingly. A second unexpected blow was the discovery that the County Council had not arranged any "11 Plus" entry during the last year as a grammar school. Fortunately some local parents found this out – before the governors – and appealed to the Secretary of State who overruled the County Council. It is probably no exaggeration to say that these parents saved the school. Perhaps the governors were partly to blame for not tying things up properly with the officials in County Hall.

The first few years of independence certainly tested the new board of governors although the underlying belief, with all the teaching staff unchanged, was that things would come right. Not surprisingly the numbers on roll fell from 420 to about 370 – many parents of young girls in the area not being too sure about the future of the school. Then after about two years both the entry and the numbers staying in the sixth form began to increase. Word was getting around that the school was sound.

The governors' new role changed from one of expediency to one of getting the administration of the school onto a proper business footing. Little had been spent on the buildings for years and as in all secondary schools there was a growing need for more space and special facilities. The cost would run into millions. Gradually an administrative policy was evolved which can be summarised as follows:

a   The running of the school and the organising of the teaching were the responsibility of the Headmistress. There was to be no doubt about that.

b   The first charge on the budget would be the requirements of the Headmistress (In practice nothing was ever refused)

c   There being no loan charges, the fees could be kept low and still produce a small surplus for capital expenditure. (There was a difference of opinion on this matter. In a normal business undertaking money would be borrowed from the bank to provide all the required facilities immediately and the debt gradually paid off, out of revenue. The opposite opinion was to make do with the facilities as they were and put aside any surplus for a "rainy day". In the event the governors took a middle course of paying for capital expenditure out of revenue – neither borrowing nor saving up revenue.)

d   The Bursar would act as Clerk to the Governors as well as being the Headmistress's principal administrative officer, on the strict understanding that the paperwork for the governors must be kept to a minimum – ten percent of his time being the suggested proportion. The governors sought advice from other schools and "educationalists" on this subject and were warned that "empire building" on office work could easily get out of hand. There was one lurid description of a board "sinking under the weight of its own pomposity!"

e   The planning of the school development and the design of many new buildings would be done by a qualified ARIBA architect and not by a builder's draughtsman. The aim was to add a new building every two years, work starting at the beginning of the summer holidays so as to get the noisy part done before the girls reassembled for the Autumn term.

Things went well – the increase in the number of girls being the main reason – and the governors' meetings became quite exciting. Members actually looked forward to discussing the next moves. Each project was first considered by a working party of the Chairman, Headmistress, Bursar, Architect, Head of Department and one or two of the Assistant Teachers. Sketch designs were then prepared and finally a full design and estimate produced for the approval of the governors. The programme went according to plan except that the much needed Music Centre had to be put back to make way for the new "in" subject of Technology. The Sports Hall was a particular problem. The "package-deals" offered by several firms were tempting but none of them looked right and in the end the school architect designed one large enough to accommodate four badminton courts. From all accounts a very successful undertaking.

Early in the 1980's the new government started the Assisted Places Scheme – in effect means tested scholarships for able children of parents on low incomes. The governors liked the idea but did not wish to become too dependent on this source of income and agreed to 15 per cent. of the entry being "assisted" in this way. In practice this proved about right. In Surrey there were surprisingly few girls of the required ability with parents on incomes low enough to derive any real help from the scheme.

So in less than a decade some £2.5 million worth of building had been done (its present value being at least twice that amount); the number on the roll had risen from under 400 to nearly 600; no debt had been incurred; the fees had been kept comparatively low; and the examination results had established Sir William Perkins's School in the top flight of independent girl's schools.

The governors had reason to be satisfied with this work but the real credit must go to the Headmistresses and their loyal staff, who, by achieving such good results attracted not only the parents of young girls with the necessary ability but also teachers of the highest professional standing. The school can now only look forward.

Recollections of Going Independent

Mrs Alison Millard, Head of the English Department, recalls how the staff coped with a difficult period of change.

When I joined the staff of Sir William Perkins's School in 1969, it was clear that change was to be expected, though Surrey had not yet made much progress towards ending selection at eleven, not least because of its policy of keeping its secondary schools small. This had been effective, producing in the main well managed institutions, each with a distinct identity, where staff and pupils all knew one another. However, the problem then arose of how they could be combined or enlarged to produce schools large enough to provide for the varied needs of the full ability range. This was certainly true of the Chertsey, Egham and Addlestone area, which possessed a small grammar school for girls, Sir William Perkins's School, one for boys, Strodes at Egham, and two co-educational secondary modern schools, The Meads in Chertsey and St Pauls in Addlestone, none being close enough to the any other to create even a split-site school.

Nevertheless, Surrey was committed to reorganisation, so a plan was devised in, I think, 1976, whereby Strodes would become the Sixth Form College, fed by a single school on The Meads and St Pauls sites (with a level-crossing in between!) Sir William Perkins's School would be topped and tailed, in other words lose its Sixth Form and receive no new intake whilst the existing population grew out. When all that remained amounted to what we now know as years 10 and 11, the remaining pupils would join their peers and the Sir William Perkins's School site would close.

We all believed that this was a plan designed to be unacceptable. There was no real place for Sir William Perkins's School in any scheme that Surrey could devise, yet the other schools could not at that time have accommodated an additional 250 pupils if we had closed. Surrey needed us to leave the LEA. We had had voluntary controlled status since 1948. The question was whether in 1978 we could afford to go out of the state system and revert to being a wholly independent school.

In principle, this could be done. Because the trustees owned the land, the buildings erected in the 1950's did not have to be paid for. (The Royal Grammar School in Guildford had to purchase what had been built on Surrey-owned land when it reverted to being an independent school). However, anything 'unfixed' that Surrey had provided over the thirty years had to be bought; every desk, every ink-stained text book, every rounders bat, every test tube – and even the plastic washing up bowl in the staff pantry – would be valued by the county's assessors and the bill presented. Where was the money to come from? Who was to make all this happen?

The people who did it were, above all, the Head, Miss Betty Timbrell, the Deputy Head, Miss Eleanor Littleboy, and the Governors, led by Mr Peall. Miss Timbrell and Mr Peall had much in common: they found themselves called upon to perform a huge range of tasks they had never foreseen, to take risks that were alien to all their previous experience and to shoulder responsibilities that must have seemed awe-inspiringly weighty. That they undertook this all is greatly to their credit and that they succeeded so entirely is magnificent. They achieved what became the school as it is now through integrity, attention to detail and unremitting hard work over a number of years. They trusted each other and they were themselves entirely trustworthy and that made all the difference.

Where did the money come from? Some of it the trustees had, though not much. Some of it came from Surrey, who had to pay fees for girls who had entered the school when it belonged to the LEA, but only until they were sixteen. The Sixth Form had to be paid for by parents and for the first few years many left after "O" levels. Some of it was raised by individuals: Mrs Kimmins, then as now a governor, went out and about to companies with funds available to make charitable gifts for educational purposes and gained donations for scholarships; Miss Sames, the previous Headmistress, endowed a scholarship; a professional fundraiser was engaged, through whose work former pupils learned of our needs and gave generously, as did charitable organisations.

Some of the money came from the dead, when the school's treasures, gifts of our benefactors, were sold. The Tulk China went to the sale room and we gasped when we learned what the pretty things we passed every day in their showcases in the corridors were actually worth. Furniture went too, including the Headmistress's desk, and the ornate mirror outside her study door at which staff and pupils alike checked the tidiness of their hair before going in to see her proved to be quite remarkably valuable. Somehow, enough came in to keep the show on the road.

The staff did their bit, too, mainly by staying on. Surrey had an obligation to relocate any of its employees who wished to remain with the LEA, but nearly all of us preferred to take our chances with the new school, though several people who would have gone anyway, for promotion, to take up posts in other parts of the country or to start their families, did leave.

We all spent the last day of the Summer Term attaching sticky labels marked 'SWPS' to any item of furniture or equipment that pre-dated 1948 so that the assessors from Surrey who came in during the holidays did not charge for it. Some of it is still in use.

Something we had never had to do before was to acquire pupils. In the past, girls had sat the 11 Plus and Surrey had sent us sixty of these every September. We advertised an Entrance Examination, held it appallingly late in the year, in March, and waited to see if anyone came to sit it. A fair number did, so, knowing no better, we arranged tables in the hall as for 'O' levels and were surprised and dismayed by how intimidating the youthful candidates found it.

We set our own English and Maths papers, which were taken in the morning. The number of entrants was so small that we asked them to bring a packed lunch. We provided hot soup in the HE Room and there were activities including a keep-fit session in the gym as well as a quiet time in the library. In the afternoon they sat a verbal Reasoning test which we had bought in. ("It's an interesting paper," said the eleven year old Emma Dinwiddy kindly." I've answered it at two other Entrance Exams…") Many staff and senior girls came in to help, a custom which survives to this day, and teachers of all subjects took home Verbal Reasoning papers to mark, leaving the English and Maths staff free to cope with their own papers. The academic standard of entry was high and a large number of the places offered was accepted.

Out of all this came Sir William Perkins's Independent School for Girls, which opened its doors in September 1978. Its first year was on the small side and its sixth form was tiny, but we were alive and well. There were troubled times in the early years, such as the sudden tragic death of the school's first bursar, Colonel James (he was known to the girls as 'the pin-striped wonder', because of his energy and unfailing good humour and immaculate tailoring!) Mr Peall acted as bursar, unpaid) pro-tem – as well as Chief Electrician (also unpaid)! Money was very tight until the numbers, particularly in the sixth form, had time to build up.

For me, those early days of the independent school were amongst my happiest. True, the building was a little scruffy and lacked all but the essential maintenance; the temporary classrooms, or 'chalets' as we called them, never 'huts', were viciously cold in winter and airless in summer; the P E staff got by somehow in a minute gymnasium, now the ground floor of the Art building; Miss Heaney and her classes performed wonders in an ill-equipped Art Room, now Rooms 10 and 11; when you gave out a set of text books you always took along a roll of sellotape: there was no money for anything that was not essential. We stayed because we liked it and because we liked and respected one another. Also, we believed in what we were doing. "One day," said Miss Ruth Allott, then Head of Classics, "they will want excellence again. It is the job of people like us, who know how to encourage it, to keep the lamps alight". And so it proved to be.

It is often remarked that the true motto of Sir William Perkins's School is "Look upon it as a challenge". I have uttered that sentence countless times down the years, grimly, cynically, facetiously, with all possible inflections, but never without remembering that in 1978 that is exactly what we did – and we overcame.

A Head's Task becomes Formidable

Miss Betty Timbrell was Headmistress from 1971 – 1981

Miss Timbrell voiced some of her personal reactions to the prolonged struggle for the school's survival in her annual speeches as Prize Giving. Her remarks were particularly poignant because they always followed glowing reports of the school's continuing academic successes and lively activities.

In 1973, after the County had proposed the loss of the sixth form:

"Living in troubled times, with our school facing an uncertain future we would do well to remember that, in the year in 1914, the problems which faced the newly formed school must have seemed just as daunting. The first Headmistress, Miss Eastaugh, and the school accepted the challenge of their generation and I hope that we shall meet our future with equal courage…"

It was in this spirit that the staff determined to embark on an ambitious programme of events to celebrate 250 years of the school's history in 1975. A Thanksgiving Service was held in Guildford Cathedral, over 400 former pupils and staff attended a reunion weekend, the Surrey County Magazine published an article about the school by Miss Littleboy and there was a special anniversary edition of 'The Rambler'. One or two elderly visitors to the celebrations had themselves been pupils at the voluntary elementary school on the site and remembered its closure in 1908. That this successful grammar school might also now be closed seemed a particularly unjust turn of fate.

Miss Timbrell's 1976 report ended with these words….

"… Shortly after we had finished celebrating our 250th Anniversary members of the County Council announced their decision to seek to close the school. At about the same time came the news that for financial reasons Surrey must lose 3 to 400 teachers, and this was soon to be followed by rumours of possible redundancy in the future. Information of this kind can have such a devastating effect on a staff that a Head's task becomes a formidable one. The account I have just given shows clearly that the staff here have not lost their enthusiasm – in any way at all – and I can assure you that it is from their loyal support and capacity for work and from their frequent good humour and merriment, that I have drawn my strength. And as I thank them sincerely for all that they do I should also like to take this opportunity to thank especially Miss Littleboy who, as Deputy Head – has perhaps the most difficult job of all… We believe that just as the astronaut stepped with courage from his cabin into the unknown so when the time comes, we must, as a school move confidently from the maintained into the independent sector."

The important step into independence was taken in September 1978. By 1979 Miss Timbrell's annual speech was full of optimism.

"… You have heard from Mr Peall this afternoon of the Governors' plan for a major expansion. This September we were pleased to welcome three First Year forms and we shall continue to offer 75 places each year to suitable candidates. We have 400 pupils at the present time and we anticipate that the size of the school when fully expanded with be approximately 450… In place of that rather uncertain confidence that was with us in September 1978 we have established a real and lasting strength."

'The Last of the Grammar School Girls'

Sir William Perkins's School 1977 – 84 by Sarah Stocker

As a year group, we have always felt rather distinctive (or perhaps that should be notorious). Despite the enormous changes in the School's status and funding during the move to independence, we were conscious of little happening at ground level. However, we were aware that we had an opportunity to take advantage of an SWPS education that probably for many of us would not have been possible without the 11 plus. Occasionally, we were aggrieved as we felt those who followed us had greater privileges due to their fee paying status. This was balanced by a sense of smugness that our places were due solely to our personal academic prowess. Junior lunch times seemed the most common time for little spats to break out between the respective year groups. As we were responsible for serving, any disrespect to the third years could be punished by smaller portions.

Ironically, we came very close to not attending SWPS at all. The year that we were due to take the 11 plus, it was mysteriously and disappointingly cancelled. Then, just as mysteriously, it appeared several months later for one final outing. Many us were quite indignant that the boys were not made to take these tests and we knew something significant was happening as we were handed new pencils each time. There seemed to be a preponderance of questions concerning policemen.

If PC 'A' has big feet, PC 'B' has a panda car PC 'C' works nights etc which one rides a bicycle and gets home in time for tea?

Once the letters from the Education department arrived and had been interpreted, the trip to Hawkins for uniforms was a significant occasion. We were fitted out with the standard uniform, including the very expensive gabardine raincoats with the huge epaulettes, rarely worn more than once or twice. Also very unpopular were the dog tooth checks of the summer uniform and the iniquitous pursebelts, which when filled with small change (for Toffee Pops) sat very unflatteringly and added bulges to our waistlines. There were shrill maternal complaints about French navy A line skirts that bobbled immediately from the rough underside of our desks. Ours was the era of the very short fat tie, so short and fat that it could barely form itself into a knot. We all wore long fringes which flicked up over one eye at an alarming angle. Later, by the sixth form we all had very big hair - huge high - maintenance perms.

We settled into school life quickly and although many of us had come from very modern primary schools we felt quite secure in the old buildings with their sense of history and tradition. Many staff members have a lasting influence over the course of our lives but who can fail to remember dear Miss Daniel, who would whiz along the front drive on her moped, in her knitted trouser suit, with books clutched between her knees and a priceless antiquarian vase from Chertsey Museum strapped to the rear pannier ?

At an early age we were clear about the school's academic focus and we had the impression that sport was not seen as a significant area of the curriculum. In comparison to the facilities offered today, freezing February mornings in the old gym were not a welcoming prospect, as we had to get changed in the main school and run out to the front of the building in shorts. Aertex shirts would often be rigid with the cold and had to be beaten into submission to make them pliable enough to wear. Athletics often meant pleasant half hours sitting in the summer sun, chatting around the long jump, until one of the PE staff came into view, at which point we all sprang to attention. Tennis was much more popular. There was always a rush on summer mornings to use the court directly behind the main building, in fact we used to get into school earlier and earlier, sometimes catching trains at 6.30am to pip others at the post.. Those girls selected for special coaching for the squad were regarded with envy as the rest of us were left 'knocking up', 8 to a court.

By the sixth form we were trusted to pursue more independent activities. Occasionally, this trust was sadly abused. One of the choices was to go to Staines swimming pool. During a spot check at the pool, there was only one lone sixth former ploughing up and down. It came to light that the slips given to SWPS swimmers to register attendance had been collected in bulk (on a rota basis) and distributed the following morning, leaving the rest of us free to pursue leisure activities of our own choosing on a Wednesday afternoon. Later on, golf was a popular choice. The fact that the tutor was a youngish gentleman obviously was not lost on participants.

The time of entry into the lower sixth in 1982 was a very significant period, both for the girls and the school. Surrey County Council had only paid our fees until the end of the fifth form and we were offered the opportunity of transferring to Strodes College for A level studies. It was a tempting time to move - a chance for us to experience co-educational study in an apparently more liberal environment without the need for a significant financial input from our parents. However, it was extremely important for the school to establish a strong 6th form. The very generous bursaries overcame for many people the temptations of sixth form college. Certainly feelings of loyalty and being valued by the school were also significant. Most of us experienced a sigh over what might have been but comforted ourselves with the knowledge this was really much better for us educationally and that our rewards would come later in life.

There are fond memories of the old sixth form centre, despite its shortcomings in terms of accommodation provision. It was far too small for the number of occupants so eleven of us used to huddle into a room about 6ft square, several sitting under the table. If anyone wanted to leave, we all used to have to evacuate the room. The allocation of rooms was an unknown equation but we certainly did not stray into territory not belonging to us. It felt extremely mature to make our own hot drinks, although this was not allowed during lesson time. This was generally accepted, particularly as Miss Allott could see directly from her classroom to the kitchen area.

The Christmas sixth form revues and pantomimes were thoroughly enjoyed by the lower school. These seemed increasingly more risqué, and one memorable year, the lower sixth 'arranged' for an apparently famous pop star to make a guest appearance. He was mobbed by adoring crowds as he stepped from the car at the school gates, some were even able to glimpse his blue suede shoes. This was perhaps regarded as the thin end of the wedge, words were obviously had, and subsequent shows were rather more subdued. I recall a strong sense that as members of the school, we were expected to behave with dignity. On this occasion, standards were obviously seen to slip.

School trips were quite an occasion. These started locally (Merrist Wood and Fishbourne Roman Palace) and progressed further afield. In the fourth year, we took a trip to Brittany, staying with local families. We were a highly visible group as most of us were kitted out in identical long white net scarves from a well known department store.

On one memorable occasion, the coach driver left us by the side of the road for a picnic and didn't return for hours. We were all imagining the headlines. The Sixth form Cruise in 1982 was around the Mediterranean on the SS Uganda. It had just finished serving after the Falklands War, and it appeared to have had all the luxury trimmings removed *after* it was used to transport Argentinian prisoners of war. Despite the basic conditions and the ferocious crew, it was a memorable trip, particularly visiting Bethlehem on Christmas Day.

In common with today's school , the community ethic was very strong. We appreciated the privileges we enjoyed and enormous efforts went into form charity fundraising. In particular, we enjoyed very positive links with Botleys Park residents.

Looking back over our school years, we were always conscious of a very strong focus on the curriculum, with less emphasis on subjects we felt were seen as 'extras' such as art, music and sport. We had a suspicion that these were considered more suitable for people who couldn't manage the full academic range of 'options' at the end of their third year.

Although we only left school fifteen years ago, many of us feel that the school then was much more similar in appearance and outlook to that of previous decades than to today's SWPS. Realistically, this is probably connected to higher levels of financial investment and more advanced facilities, but I think also reflects more modern educational trends.

In contrast to today, there appeared little concept of school preparing us directly for working life. There seemed few links with industry, commerce or technology and little emphasis on vocational training. Our business was to be getting to university. There would be plenty of time to think about careers later. These were the times when less than 5% of the population went on to further education, so a straightforward academic degree would open all the doors necessary.

Our memories are of a school with great academic traditions which we were proud to follow, whilst at the same time having a little kick against the traces, wherever possible. Many lasting friendships were forged and most importantly, we also were inspired with a really genuine sense of 'feminism' - there were no barriers to what we could achieve in the world ahead. Perhaps, on reflection, we have more in common with today's SWPS girls than we initially thought.

The School Grows
Anne Darlow - Headmistress from 1982 – 1994

The school had been independent for three years when I joined in January 1982 and I was fortunate to find a deputy like Miss Littleboy to ease me into its ways.

On that first morning builders were upstairs finishing off new offices for the bursar so I occupied a temporary home with the filing cabinets behind the main office. From there I looked out at the newly completed Tulk classrooms though at the time I could not have foreseen the immense building programme the Governors would undertake in the next thirteen years: the Brunner and Eastaugh blocks, a sports hall, sixth form common room and art centre conversions, a technology workshop, biology laboratories and a centre for music and drama.

I have some sympathy with two visiting Old Girls who would have preferred to see only the school they remembered as pupils and pointed out that good teachers mattered more than new buildings. However applicants for teaching posts as well as prospective parents examined our facilities with a critical eye. The 1892 gymnasium without a changing room, its limited space lined with wall bars, had clearly been designed for a gentler Victorian regime of exercise. There was a 1950's feel to the domestic science room. The scrubbed wooden draining boards and table tops were unfamiliar to parents accustomed to built in kitchens, much though they might have liked their daughters taught to clean the bath and make the bed in the adjoining home craft flat. If it could be avoided the tour did not include the sixth form common room in the most remote of the wooden chalets though I suspect that the girls were less alarmed than the staff by its bouncing floor and evidence of mouse visitors. By 1982 the life span of most of the temporary classrooms was nearly at an end and before long there were other pressures on the existing buildings.

A succession of radical changes followed close on the heels of school reorganisation. New examination and assessment systems which often affected teaching methods, the National Curriculum and the relentless advance of technology. In 1982 the Parents' Association presented the school with a laser printer for 'the' computer. Within two years a computer room had been built and equipped for class teaching. Thereafter machines in increasing numbers and applications invaded most subject departments and the administration. The early transition period was embarrassing for some of us as the young often knew more than their seniors. I struggled painfully through work sheets that the first year pupils took in their stride.

The girls usually relished the developments which gave them 'hands on' experience not only with computers, but with scientific experiments in the laboratories and in design technology. The scope for constructing models to test their designs was limited in a classroom but when the technology workshop opened the girls set to work sawing and drilling, hammering and soldering with enthusiasm. Calls for the first aid box were fewer than the pessimists had forecast but twelve girls kept a teacher fully occupied. More space, equipment and staff time were needed to deliver the curriculum.

The sports hall and the centre for music and drama were particularly ambitious projects though no one doubted that they were deserved by departments that contributed so much to school life. The whole school community was involved in fund raising and the parents were generous in their response to the appeal launched by our enterprising, ex-naval bursar, Commander Allfrey. When the sports hall was opened we had the extraordinary experience of moving overnight through a hundred years from the old gymnasium to the most modern facilities. The pupils who were there in 1988 may remember it with the same excitement that Miss Schumacher's mother felt when she entered the 1892 building.

Many girls are likely to recall a special match or dramatic or musical performance as the highlight of their school careers.

It was always hard when a production that had been rehearsed for months came to an end and the wonderful sets were dismantled. The revival of the school magazine in 1982 ensured that some of the outstanding art work and creative writing will be preserved in the archives along with eye-witness accounts of the school activities. The challenge of the Duke of Edinburgh's Award Scheme proved surprisingly popular. The code of conduct for weekend expeditions, mostly kept by the girls and invariably by the staff assessors, was that however much it rained and however dispirited the team, everyone should be at school on time on Monday morning. Without the gallant band of parents who trained as helpers to share these feats of endurance far fewer girls would have won their awards. Sixth formers also recognised the important business skills they could develop in Young Enterprise. I still have a varied collection of items to remind me of the persuasiveness of the sales staff of the different companies.

Pupil numbers grew steadily and it says much for the reputation of Miss Timbrell and the staff had established for the school that there were so many applications for places. The 1980's was, after all, a period of demographic change when the number of secondary school pupils was falling. There were also years of economic recession when jobs were insecure and many parents could not contemplate fees for education. The Assisted Places Scheme provided a way in for a few girls but for many more it was a matter of parents tightening belts and making sacrifices once they had decided that this was the right school. There were many different lines of enquiry to establish this, but I particularly remember a father asking what I would do if his daughter appeared in school one morning with green hair. Fortunately, she did not put me to the test.

In 1990 1Q joined forms 1L, 1M and 1P as a fourth form of entry. The sixth form numbers were also rising. With 130 of them on the register another round of planning applications began, but this time the staff as well as the sixth form were to get the new study and common rooms they needed.

There can be little doubt that the school's academic record has always played an important part in attracting pupils, but when the first 'league tables' published in the Sunday Times placed Sir William Perkins's School in the list of the top 30 independent schools in the country, it achieved recognition that might not otherwise have come the way of a little known former grammar school. A good education however cannot be measured by statistics and the Old Girls were nearer the truth when they emphasised good teachers. In that respect and in its Chairmen of Governors this school has great strength. Mr Peall, Col Jarvis, Mrs Kimmins and Miss Mark have all given expertise and wisdom, unswerving support and unlimited time to the school. When Miss Ross stepped into my shoes I was glad that in Mrs Phillips she too would inherit a kind and experienced deputy head to help her.

32 A corner of the sixth form common room 1984.

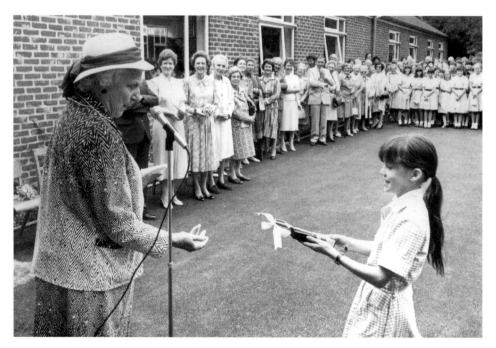

33 Miss Sames formally opens the Brunner Buildings 1984.

34 The SWPS entry in Chertsey's Black Cherry Fair 1984.

35 School production of 'Twelfth Night' 1991.

36 School production of 'The King and I' 1992.

Life in the Sixth Form 1992 - 1994

Elaine Pratt was elected Head Girl by her fellow sixth formers.

Life as a sixth former between 1992 and 1994 provided a girl with many privileges. The main source of these rights stemmed from the exclusive use of the Sixth Form Centre, a mystery to the younger members of the school who were strictly prohibited from setting foot beyond "the Double Doors". The centre was located, as it is today, at the rear of the school, as an afterthought attached to the H E Room. It comprised as follows:

The Quiet Room – where a girl could study during her treasured free periods, albeit that she was surrounded by burgeoning lockers, paper and text-book strewn wooden shelves, lunch boxes and the contents of several sports bags. This room was multi-purposed. Used for registration, socialising, storage of stage props, costumes and scenery and host to the odd hysterical outburst by senior pupils prior to exams, performances and driving tests, one wonders how it acquired its name.

The Common Room – this provided a haven for the senior pupil to relax. A light and airy space, with windows on three sides and sporting a colourful mural on the fourth. The abundance of natural daylight brought with it sub-zero temperatures in winter due to the slight warping of the antique metal window frames and a similarly aged heating system. Any attempt to warm this room was always welcomed and it has since been debated as to whether this inspired the rainforest mural which appeared in 1992 (thanks to the efforts of Mr McKillop and some budding sixth form artists), covering the entire surface of the one glass free wall – no door, skirting board or piece of covering was spared.

The common room also contained a kitchen where a girl could make a cup of tea or coffee, a warm lunch on a cold day or an early morning pot noodle as a breakfast supplement. Despite being fully equipped with formica cupboards and drawers, some of which had doors and handles (of varying shades of white and beige) crockery and cutlery were scarcely found within the confines of the "breakfast bar" compound. For reasons unbeknown to many, users preferred to scatter implements throughout the two rooms, predominantly on tables and the foam filled comfy chairs. Samples for 'A' level micro-biology projects were in great supply, particularly when the syllabus dictated the study of fungi. The implementation and enforcement of a kitchen duty rota was pursued ad nauseum by the Head Girls; inevitably this met with little success. However, there is little room for doubt that this charming characteristic of the Common Room was instilled from its opening, years ago, continuing ceaselessly until its demolition in 1994.

Alongside a girl's coffee mug could be found various belongings ranging from science laboratory coats to a cardboard cut out of Bart Simpson. The lab coats were not, of course, the regulation school blue but white, a privilege embraced by most sixth formers who had chosen to pursue sciences at 'A' level. These coats were recognisable by their personal grafitti and the choice of velcro or press-stud fastening. Traditionally lab coats fastened by a knot tie at the waist; however, such fastenings were replaced following an unfortunate warming experience for a GCSE chemistry student who made contact with the escaped contents of a test tube during a "practical". Whilst, thankfully, nobody was hurt, school policy was changed in favour of quick release in emergencies!

In return for these privileges, sixth formers were expected to adopt certain responsibilities.

Thursday mornings often gave rise to a tense atmosphere in the Quiet Room. Staff meetings necessitated sixth form prefects to supervise junior classes, taking the register and generally keeping noise levels to a low din. A girl's approach to this task was often determined by the year group in which her junior class was currently residing. Those attending first and second year classes were often smiling in anticipation of their enthusiastic welcome by adoring juniors. The third and fourth year designates were often ashen faced and perspiring slightly at the thought of entering rooms filled with recently teenaged girls eager to practice their newly acquired skills of self assertion. Prefects headed for the fifth form corridor were few and far between. The few who felt duty bound to attend were resigned to the fact that, if acknowledged at all, their reputation would be at best, cold. The register would be completed by guess-work and a little courage.

Less traumatic responsibilities involved staffing the tuck shop at first rec. This occupation became less hazardous for girls than their predecessors when the low level barriers formed by the tuck-shop cabinets were replaced by a fully reinforced shed, behind which Highland Toffees and Fizzy Lizzies could be sold at arms length from the sugar-crazed hoards. To further counter any healthy eating policies of the catering staff, the sixth form sale of doughnuts on a Friday was introduced. All profits went to charity, as did a well stocked tray to the staff room!

Senior pupils were encouraged to broaden their outlook and partake in extra-curricular activities. Sporty types became heavily involved in training sessions and playing for the first VII and XI; Wearing school colours and travelling far and wide to successfully compete in county and national level tournaments and returning victorious on many occasions whilst less athletic girls looked on in bewilderment from their comfy chairs and chip butties (I can say this as I was one of the bewildered ones!).

For the profit-minded there was the opportunity to set up and run a company under the Young Enterprise Scheme. Weekly board meeting at and support from a local engineering company spurred the production of material bags and accessories. These efforts took the 18 member strong company to successful heights in the regional competition. Members of the "Anon" production team were able to develop their artistic skills in the use of sewing machines and accessory design. In the absence of appropriate equipment, girls showed initiative and the ability to adapt. Needless to say, many kitchen implements remain, to this day, an attractive damson colour following the fashionable "tie-dye" approach to bag decoration.

Opportunities for thespians were vast. Script writing, production and directions was inherent in the Junior Drama competition. First and second year classes battled it out between one another hoping to prove their sixth form team had written and produced the best 20 minute production. Amazingly, performances were of a high calibre, despite strikes and sit-ins by junior members during a number of rehearsals. Persuasion and bribery were unashamedly used to fill the ever popular staff "cameo" roles in the sixth form panto. However, the highlight of the 1993 dramatic year was the school production of Hamlet following the proverbial blood, sweat and tears and a large proportion of the common room being given over to stage scenery and props.

Those looking for a vocation or just a different perspective on life signed up for community service. Visiting pensioners in the local sheltered housing complex or working with handicapped children at the White Lodge Centre inspired many a young mind, with ancillary benefits of endless supplies of tea and rock buns and avoiding Wednesday assembly.

Girls were also encouraged to develop their debating skills through a series of political discussions and Tuesday afternoon lectures. Memorable speakers ranged from members of the Anti-Nazi league to Buddhist Monks. Local politicians were quizzed and challenged on many contentious issues, with the devil's advocate making an appearance on a weekly basis.

The acquisition of driving licences and cars of varying reliability improved senior pupils' social lives significantly. Local haunts were The Anchor at Pyrford and Thames Court at Shepperton, hosting post exam/results celebrations. The Riverside Club at Chertsey Bridge was the favoured venue for sixth form parties. Whilst under the guise of raising money for charity, the underlying purpose was to provide endless hours of excited chatter before and after the event.

During my seven years at Perks, the school underwent some aesthetic changes both internally and externally. The old gym, used for P E lessons involving apparatus, climbing ropes and a few concussion injuries, was converted into the new art studio. A much larger and well equipped sports hall was constructed and opened in 1988; pupils and parents sponsoring bricks to contribute to the funds. The library was extended, consuming an old form room (9) to accommodate the careers library and the increasing number of girls who stayed for prep.

Metal lockers were introduced gradually, replacing the traditional wooden lift-up desks.

The music centre was under construction as I left in 1994 and shortly after the "chilly haven" was replaced by an impressive double glazed facility.

I, like many of my "Old Girl" friends have fond memories of life at Perks. Over time the unforgettable (if not humbling) experiences of the annual summer P E Challenge of the 1500 meters (10 minutes was my personal best) or the forgotten works of Shakespeare whilst performing Twelfth Night never cease to raise a smile.

Great days!

37 The Tuck Shop.

38 The Staff on Mufti Day 1992. Mrs Miller, Miss Davies, Mrs Wright, Mrs Lamont, Mr Mitchell, Mrs Graham, Mrs Bolton, Mrs Sutton, Dr Mason, Mrs Taylor, Mrs Evans, Mrs Dodson (in background), Miss Gomez, Miss Bramwell, Mr Jaundrill, Mrs Miles, Mrs Bendall, Mrs Greenslade, Mr McKillop, Mrs Ogilvie, Mrs Robinson, Mrs Holdaway and Mrs Millard.

39 The Senior Sixth 1994.

Postscript 1994 –

My first sight of the school was on a damp and very misty day in November 1993, when I came for interview. The grey and cold of the exterior surroundings was soon dispelled by the warmth of the welcome and, instinctively, I knew it was the 'right place'.

Arriving officially in September 1994 I was following in the footsteps of Anne Darlow with continuous change and development. For the first term the teaching staff had to 'camp out' in Room 5 whilst the staff room was rebuilt and extended. The end result was a vast improvement in working conditions, well deserved after the cramped and limited space previously available.

The Governor's vision continued with plans to provide an ICT centre, enlarge and improve the sixth form centre and provide new modern language facilities. One of the most popular developments was the provision of an enclosed entrance lobby to the Main School Hall. Now that it is possible to enter the Hall from within the building, there is far less 'dusting down' after Assembly and a much warmer wait for late comers to evening events.

However, it is not just in buildings that the school has changed. Girls have been involved in an enormous range of activities. The German exchange with the St. Georg Gymnasium in Bocholt, continues to flourish and new ventures such as visits to the Sinai and the Holy Land have been introduced. The Duke of Edinburgh's Award Scheme has produced offshoots such as 'Manoeuvres in the Dark'. The list of sports undertaken at every level, from beginner to national standard, has continued to grow and music and drama have flourished. There is something for everyone from the UK mathematics challenge to the Public Speaking Competition.

The most rewarding part of the last few years has been the working together of so many; the pupils, staff, parents, FOSWPS, governors. Their support, commitment and enthusiasm have been invaluable.

As the School looks to the 21st Century it can do so with confidence, having taken the best from the past to build a school equipped and ready for the new millennium and able to produce confident young women, prepared for the excitement and challenge of the world of the future.

Susan Ross
Headmistress